From Ups and Downs to Middle Ground

Surviving Bipolar

Brandi Rae Blouch

Audrey -
looking forward to
possibilities.

Brandi Blouch

To contact the author, visit
Nourishyoursweetspot.com

Library of Congress Control Number:2018900964

Create Space Independent Publishing Platform, North Charleston, SC

Title # 7349218

IBSN-10: 1978176260

ISBN-13: 9781978176263

Printed in the United States of America

Reviews

"Brandi's story is inspiring and enlightening. She is a great example of what happens when you take ownership of everything that you are and the life-saving benefits of self-care and self-advocacy. All of us experience ups and downs but finding an equilibrium between extremes is what separates the sick-mind from the well. Kudos to Brandi for bravely stepping into the limelight to explain that, and then asking that the houselights get turned on. May your mission help the millions who have been in the dark-those that are afflicted by mood disorders, the people who care for them and the systems that perpetuate their illness."   Marj Clark, Booking Agent

"Get Booked....Get Business"

"From Ups and Downs to Middle Ground, Surviving Bipolar Disorder is a raw, honest, and insightful description of Brandi's journey toward health. Her memoire reads like a conversation between close friends. She is gentle, yet real regarding the everyday struggles people with Bipolar and their loved one's face. Her memoire gives readers understanding and hope. This book is a useful and approachable read for anyone interested in understanding and managing bipolar disorder."

Pamela McGuire, MSW, LCSW

Dedication

I dedicate this book to those who suffer from mental illness in silence.

I dedicate this to my family who never gave up on me. I could not have survived all I went through without your love and strength, and guidance.

For those who have believed in me even when I had doubt.

My love, you gave me the best gift when you gave me your heart. You have loved me unconditionally through the ups and downs and in between. You never judged me or made me feel less . Our love will carry us through this life and all the ones after. You are mine forever and always.

Table of Contents

"….Something very beautiful happens to people when their world has fallen apart; a humility, a nobility, a higher intelligence emerges at just the point when our knees hit the floor"

Marianne Williamson

Preface

When I was given my formal diagnosis, I was told I had Bipolar Disorder I, with rapid cycling and PTSD. I originally had many questions but didn't know what to ask because I didn't know what I didn't know. The doctor gave me a prescription for a mood stabilizer along with an antidepressant. I had a lot to learn.

I learned that bipolar was passed along genetically. I also learned that my environment can trigger my symptoms. There is a genetic link that hangs around awaiting a trigger to make it active. The rapid cycling means that my moods can fluctuate from an elevated mood of mania to a depression very quickly. Moods usually take days to weeks to cycle. Those of us with rapid cycling do so much quicker. This can also cause more havoc more quickly.

I was also told that I have PTSD (Post Traumatic Stress Disorder) from experiences I had in my childhood. For years I experienced behaviors and memories that didn't make much sense. One thing is I startle very easily. I startle so easily that my nephew and niece find it funny to hide behind a door and jump out at me. It is funny, but I feel a strange fear deep down. I also experience screenshot like pictures of my past. This wasn't always the case. There were memories that had been pushed back so far that it took another trauma to trigger my memories of an earlier time in my life.

When I was a child of the age 4 I was sexually abused by a boy who lived across the street. Over a summer's time, many inappropriate sexual behaviors occurred. This is where the first of many traumas had begun. When that summer past so did the abuse. I can remember having other inappropriate sexual behaviors as I grew up. The first time I had sex I was 14 years old. I think the ultimate in defiant sexual behavior was me becoming a stripper.

There are times when I don't know where the darkness comes from, it arrives and lingers just long enough to throw a wrench into my life. Then I rebuild and restructure until my life seems clear and manageable again.

Interestingly, as I have written this book I have found myself with mania and a depression re-lapse. I speak about bipolar as if I am removed from it. That is not the truth. I am reminded that I do have this illness whether I like it or not. It gnaws on me like a consistent tapping on my shoulder that won't go away. The negative ideas and thoughts fill my mind. It becomes another fight for my life. What is tripping me up this time, I wonder. It is this book this time. As I have bared my heart and soul, my mind struggles to make sense of it all. I have thought thoughts and envisioned memories I thought were in the past. The disruption of my mood stability hangs on me like a heavy weight I can't shake off. I am forced to face it if I want to feel better.

Unfortunately, there are times when a walk in the darkness is needed. It is there, in the darkness, where the wounds are healed. I cry a cry that takes over my body and physically wears me out. That kind of cry makes me wonder if it will ever stop or will it take me over? My aunt always says there is a silver lining to every tragedy or whatever negativity fills your mind. I hold on to those words trusting what she says is the the truth. I continue to fight with a strength I forget I have. My strength runs deep and wide. I have to remind myself that as bad as I may feel today, it won't last forever.

As I share my ups and downs I hope you can find an inner strength you need to conquer your demons, because we all have them.

I am writing about my life, my experiences. In some areas, there are explicit details and graphic explainations of things I have been through. There may be real life stories that are difficult for some to read and not suggested for the younger readers. Please read at your discretion and know that this is my truth.

Brandi is available for speaking engagements.

You can reach her at

Nourishyoursweetspot.com

(860)410-6343

Brandi offers individual and group programs for Health Coaching

Brandi would truly appreciate a review on Amazon when you have finished reading the book.

Thank you,

Brandi Blouch

INTRODUCTION

"Insanity: Doing the same thing and expecting a different result"

Narcotics Anonymous test

pg.11

I am not my illness!! I have bipolar disorder, I am not bipolar disorder!!

You must know, you are not your illness, no matter what you have!!

You did not come across this book by accident. I do not believe in coincidences. I believe everything happens for a reason, good or bad. We are right where we are supposed to be, in this space, at this time. The universe didn't make a mistake. You found this book, you found me, for a reason.

It has taken me 10 years to learn that I am not my illness. I spent those ten years with feelings of shame, embarrassment, and guilt. I honestly believed that people knew by looking at me that I had an illness. It was somehow imprinted on my forehead for the world to read and judge. I spent this time isolated from the world around me. I have come to learn that this is one of the worst things I could have done for myself.

You or someone you know may have been suffering with or diagnosed with some form of bipolar disorder. You may or may not quite understand what that means. I am here to clear that up for you. Bipolar disorder is a mood disorder that swings high and low. This illness has its own bag of tricks.

I want you to know firstly that if you have bipolar, you do not have control over your mood swings. Many people might wonder why you don't "snap out of it". You don't because you can't, not on your own. This illness has been years in the making. You don't wake up one day with bipolar disorder. This illness has a strong genetic component as well as an environmental one. Put the two together and you have the "perfect storm".

So many of us may have struggled for many years without knowing why. There is no blood test to detect this illness, no CAT scan, or MRI. We wait until the symptoms/behaviors show up in the worst possible ways. Only then, during a crisis, do we seek out some type of help, if we are lucky. I say "lucky" because too many people commit suicide before they ever receive help or reach any type of stability.

There are many different symptoms that help doctors to diagnose this illness. Unfortunately, it can and does go undiagnosed (or is wrongly diagnosed) for years. There may be more than one illness present. This is common. There are many different pharmaceutical drugs that are used to treat this illness. Not cure it. Bipolar disorder is not one that can be cured. It can be managed with medication and different forms of therapies.

This doesn't have to be a death sentence. You can regain control of your mind and your life. You need to be diligent even when it hurts and there seems to be no reason to go on. You need to be your own advocate and fight for your life.

There are not many "go to" guides on this illness and how to get through it with your dignity intact. I did not have a guide nor did my family. We could have really used some direction that wasn't hundreds of pages long and full of medical jargon that needed to be deciphered.

I am not going to pretend that this journey is easy because it is not. Thirteen years after my diagnosis I find myself stable for the most part. I am surviving! I don't say "survived" because unfortunately, this illness is forever.

Bipolar is a life-long illness. All we can do is work and hope for is stability since there is NO cure.

In the beginning, I had no idea what I was up against, and no one prepared me. No one sat down and explained what this illness is and the gravity of what was to come.

I have put high walls around me. I have put them there because I know it is a safe place. I know I won't get hurt or be judged and my illness won't be compromised or triggered. I know that as safe as these walls feel I need to go beyond them for further growth. I slowly have started to attend events and outings. It is a process that I am committed to for the growth it will provide me. This is another thing I do to actively help myself.

I had to fight my way to stability and continue to do on a daily basis. That is how I found myself writing this book. This is my guide to surviving my illness. Too often I feel overwhelmed and not sure where to turn, or how to feel better. I have tried so many remedies and treatments before I realized that I truly needed pharmaceutical medication.

For you, your family member, your friend, or whoever has been touched by this illness, may this book help you through the ups and downs of wellness and stability.

"30 Minutes"

"I am because we all are – "

Umbatu Leymah Gbowee

The room was dark, but for the strobe lights. It smelled of stale beer along with cheap perfume, and the sweetness of the fog machine. The black lights illuminated my white dress that could be seen from across the room at the front door. That was on purpose. You would have no idea what time of year it was or even what time of day it was by looking around. It just happened to be the middle of a summer day.

Business men in button up shirts and ties filled the seats around the stage. They all had a drink of some sort in front of them, along with their single dollar bills. I could feel the vibration of my eight- inch platform shoes as they connected with the hard wood of the stage. I was supposed to be dancing, but that took too much energy. I could only saunter from one pole to the other faking my smile. It was a 30- minute set, that felt like an eternity. I couldn't find a reason to stay up there, or anywhere. I watched as the second hand moved around the clock. Every second seemed so slow, slower than normal. This didn't feel like living. I didn't feel like living. The battle in my mind was real. I was ready to get off the stage, so I could end my life, to run my car off the Sikorsky bridge. This felt like the only option and that was ok with me. Nothing mattered in that moment. I felt the dark hole that had become my life. I could find no reason to go on. I heard someone giggle and, what seemed to be out of nowhere, my niece and nephew entered my mind. I wondered if because they were so young, my death wouldn't have a lasting impact. The second hand of the clock moved so slowly. In this moment, I talked myself out of death, but only for those 60 seconds. The darkness in my soul lingered. My thoughts became a wild roller coaster ride. Up so quickly with the decent even quicker. I had no control over my thoughts. Suddenly, from a place where the light still lived, I talked myself into living, if only for 15 more seconds. Okay, I can do this, I thought. I could do this for what? What has my life become? Not one that I want. Not one that anyone would be proud of.

My sister would be devastated. I can't hurt her like this. The innocence of my niece and nephew would be robbed by me. I couldn't take that away. What right did I have to take away their childhood? But what do I really have to give? I tried to fight back the tears that rolled down my face. I was supposed to be exciting and full of sexual energy. I was the party.

I couldn't stand to look at one more man with a dollar bill in his hand. I didn't even want the money. I didn't want anything. I wanted this pain to end. The dark hole was consuming me. I had the urge to run, to leave, to get my car, that's where I wanted to be. The song changed to one that was familiar. I remember liking it, but not now.

Ten minutes remained. I tried to talk myself out of the darkness. Just when I thought I would live, I realized again that I didn't want to. There was nothing left for me to do. The second hand on the clock passed 3 and I made it 15 more seconds. I can do this, I thought, I can survive. I can make it 15 more seconds, but did I really want to? I continued to walk around the stage in disgust with what my life had become. I couldn't see a tomorrow. I couldn't see tonight.

I told myself I could get through one more minute. Then the next minute. Then 10 more seconds. Why was I doing this? Why did my mind give up on me? I wanted it to be over, whatever this is I want it to be over. I was frightened of where my thoughts were taking me. It was me against my mind's darkness and despair. I fought for a few more minutes. It was almost time to get down. My 30- minute set was just about over. I told myself If I just stayed here I will be ok. I did.

In that 30 minutes, I fought for my life. I counted the minutes by the second hand. It was the longest 30 minutes of my life. It was the biggest battle I have ever fought, the one for myself.

Childhood

"I guess, to understand what happened, and what went wrong, we must start at the beginning. The very beginning."
Unknown

We were a military family. My Dad was a career Navy Seabee. As a family, we moved about every three years within the US and abroad. We had a new place to live, new school, new friends, new social experiences, ultimately new lives.

As a young girl around age 6, my dad was either overseas with the military or on a ship. He was gone quite a lot. While he was gone my mom would often have some sort of job and she also took computer classes; she was before her time. She relied on babysitters as well as before and after school programs.

I remember going to a before school program with my sister. It was in a church across from our elementary school. We would play games with the other children until it was time to go. One of the adults would walk us across the way to school and our day would begin.

After school was a different setup. There were several kids from my street that walked home from school. I would walk with the other children home. When I would arrive, no one was home. I wore a twine rope necklace around my neck with my house key attached. I was considered and called "a latch key kid". As a "latch key kid" I knew I was coming home to an empty house. I was to tell no one. I knew there was already a prepared snack for me. I took my snack into the tv room. I ate my snack while watching Sesame Street and then Mr. Rogers Neighborhood. The TV was already on the channel I would watch; I did not have to try and find my TV shows since I didn't know how to work the television. I knew the on and off buttons, that was all. My favorite was Mr. Rogers Neighborhood. I loved the land of make believe. It was a secret place behind the walls that was accessed by a train. There were lots of colorful characters, trains, trees and flowers, even animals. I remember I would always learn some lesson or another. I learned about sharing, putting away my toys, eating my dinner. There were all sorts of hidden lessons in the land of make believe.

The summer before 4th grade my mom, sister and I moved to Newfoundland Canada, where my mom is from, from Virginia where my dad was stationed with the Navy. My Dad was in Greece working for the military for a year and we were not allowed to go with him. We already knew that when he finished there we would be moving to Japan as a family. So, since my mother wasn't going to see her extended family while we were overseas, we went to live with my Grandparents for a short period of time. I started the 4th grade in Newfoundland. It was a lot of fun. My mom is from a large family so there were always things to do. We ice skated and I got my first set of stitches. We swam, went to carnivals and regattas where I would win stuffed animals. We took hikes and would stop to eat in the wild blueberry patches. We went to the cliffs to see the Puffins in the Bird Sanctuary. There was always something fun happening.

My Dad met up with us in Newfoundland for Christmas, then we were off to Japan where nothing was ever the same.

When we arrived in Japan, we went into temporary housing on the military base. While we were there my mom was hospitalized for what we were told was "stomach problems". When she got out of the hospital her whole demeanor had changed.

 A few months later we were moved into regular base housing. We were lucky in that we got one of the attached houses of four as opposed to the high-rise apartments. We had a small flower garden in the front and some tomatoes along with the side of the building with a little back yard.

We arrived with a bang. My parents were having major marital problems, and everyone on base knew it. Ideally, my dad would have liked to start his new position uneventfully, I'm sure. Unfortunately, my mother's hospitalization seemed to be common knowledge. I think my dad was in trouble with the Captain of the base. I would over hear things once in a while.

Living on a military base was tight quarters. Everyone knew everyone else's business. Because of the close proximity to everyone I learned about things that children should not know about. Kids at school would laugh at me saying "your dad has a girlfriend". I wasn't sure what that meant for my family. I was worried and scared that my family would break up.

My mom didn't have much support so, in the beginning, she used me as a confidant. She informed me that my dad had a girlfriend in Greece and wanted to take my sister and me away to live with them. I have no idea if this was true, but It was for her. She claimed to intercept letters between my dad and his girlfriend. She once intercepted a gift. It happened to my sister's birthday. On the kitchen table sat a beautiful kabuki style Japanese doll enclosed in a glass case. My mother sat at the table with satisfaction. When my dad arrived, he saw the doll that was meant and sent (I think) to his girlfriend. I don't recall any other conversations about it and the birthday party continued.

She would also try to get me to snoop and get her information. I was only about 9-10 years old. I didn't want to do the things she asked. My dad had our passports hidden in his office, so my mother couldn't take us out of the country. One day she told me to go to my dad's office and look around and try to find the passports. I felt so scared and yucky. I didn't want to do that, at all. I slowly walked my way to his office. It was the middle of a summer day. When I arrived, my dad was in his office. I had a weird feeling that he knew what I was up to. He made no mention of it. Thankfully I didn't have to hunt around his office.

I remember I would eavesdrop on their conversations. Their arguments would wake me up. I would walk down the hall to hear what was going on. Sadly, I could hear my mom crying as my dad would tell her he no longer loved her and didn't want to be with her. He told her she could leave, but not with my sister and me. These kinds of conversations happened often.

One morning after listening to their conversation from the night before I asked my mom if dad was going to leave. She told me with tears in her eyes she didn't know. I begged her not to leave my dad until I finished school, which was light years away, I was only in the 4th grade then. She told me she wasn't sure she could make that promise. I begged and pleaded in hysterics for her to promise me she wouldn't leave until I finished school. Over and over again, getting more and more hysterical, she promised me. Looking back, I had no idea what I was asking her to promise. She had no knowledge of what was to come. I think she just held on tight and prayed.

My mother sat me down and told me that my dad wanted to take my sister and me away from her. She told me I was to always hold my sister's hand. She gave me a description of my dad's girlfriend, so I could keep a look out, and keep my sister and me safe. From there on I was constantly afraid of some strange woman trying to take us away. Play time wasn't so playful anymore.

I learned to lie quite well. After I would spend time with my dad, my mom would question me. She wanted to know what my dad had said about her. What were our conversations about? She often gave me a script of things she wanted me to say while I was with my dad. She told me to tell him that mommy loved him so much and wanted us to be a family. On my return from outings with my dad, mom wanted a recall of everything we spoke about. I lied. I never said those things to him, ever! Any responses I would tell her were a lie. I was so uncomfortable. I loved hanging out with my dad, but as time went on that time wasn't so much fun.

My mother continued to intercepted letters between my dad and his "girlfriend". After being in Japan for about 2 ½ years the base was tearing down the old temporary housing to build new ones. My mother had hidden the intercepted letters somewhere in the temporary housing walls. She wanted me to go sneak in and retrieve the letters. I told her I didn't want to, but she insisted. She told me that no one would question a child looking at the yellow caution tape and that I was to tell anyone who saw me that I was just playing. I never did it. I lied.

While in Japan my mom built a close relationship with our priest. We went to church every week. We helped with providing food and holiday items to the less fortunate. We went to a Leprosy Hospital around Christmas time and brought candy and cigarettes. We visited with those that were hospitalized and sang Christmas carols.

My mom asked our priest for help with her failing marriage. In time, our priest contacted someone on the base where my dad's girlfriend was stationed in Greece. Fraternization was not tolerated in the military.

Somehow, someway things got heated up for my dad's girlfriend and she broke off their relationship. He received a break-up letter in the mail. My parents had a huge fight that night.

I was privy to such adult matters, that needed not be. I found out by reading my mom's medical records that her "stomach ache" was not that at all. I had the desire to become a doctor, so when I came across her medical records, I was curious and read them with unknowing consequence. She was suffering from depression and had attempted suicide. My childhood was over. I lived in fear and uncertainty of what would happen to my family. Would my parents break up? Would I be separated from my sister? Would I have to live without my mom?

I no longer looked at life through bright colored lenses.

As crazy as my mother may have seemed, she fought for her man. She did not give up because she still loved him and wanted us to have an intact family. I must admire her guts, strength, and determination to fight for what she wanted.

Aside from the family drama, Japan was a fun experience. We had the freedom to go off base and go shopping by the trains. It was so safe there. There was not much crime. The Japanese people were very kind. If for some reason we got lost "they" would go out of their way to make sure we made it back ok. We experienced the culture in their festivals. We would take regular trips to see the shrines and temples. They were so beautiful. We would ride our bicycles out the back gate of the base. There was a park where we would play with other children, mostly Japanese. It was fun. The Japanese children would want to speak with us to better their english speaking skills. My sister and I really enjoyed those times.

When my sister and I were young, the moving transitions happened fairly seamlessly. As we got older they became more difficult: she and I would protest to no avail.

We moved from Japan to South Texas, Kingsville to be exact. I was about 11 years old and my sister was about 8. Again, we were in temporary housing on the base until we found a home off the base. I remember my sister and I crying most nights. That had to be difficult for my parents. Japan had been a safe place to live. There was a minimal crime. We were pretty free in a sense.

Once we moved to Texas, we were in culture shock, really. My parents had to sit us down and explain things like safety, strangers, and crime. They needed for us to know and understand that this wasn't Japan anymore. There was crime in the United States. We had to be careful about who we trusted. This was not fun for either my sister or me. We felt fear. I also think we took on my parent's fear.

Off to another school. In this middle school, I was in the minority being the only white child amongst mostly Mexican/American children. The kids here weren't very accepting, and they were out right mean. I didn't fit in. I was often concerned about whether the girls were going to beat me up like they would proclaim throughout the day. My sister wasn't having any more fun than I was (she was in elementary school). I knew this because my mom was often called to the principal's office for my sister's behavior. She often refused to take tests. She was mean to other students. She even got a pair of brass knuckles that she would take to school, just in case. She was just trying to survive the difficult situation she was dropped into. Later in life, I found out how bad it really was for her. She felt so alone. Girls would threaten her and follow her. Her bus ride across town was a daily bullying session. She eventually quit riding the bus and would walk across town to school which was a couple of miles. She didn't have much support from my parents. When she did tell my dad, his response to her was that she should fight back. No intervention or help there. Bottom line is she was bullied for years.

My dad got "us" horses. He kept them at a boarding school a bit more south. On the weekend's we would spend time there. Washing and riding the horses became an escape for my dad. We made friends with a family that lived close to where we kept the horses. To this day, my dad is still friends with them.

Then on to high school. It was a big school. It was the only high school around. It combined the two different middle school kids into one high school. It was more tolerable than middle school. I made some good friends. I enjoyed the beginning of high school. I had swim classes and diving and gymnastics. I helped teach the little kids gymnastics in an after school program. My best friend and I went to Barbizon Modeling School. We had so much fun. We "learned" how to put on makeup, walk with perfect posture, and how to take a good photo. At the end of the program, we had a fashion show. Looking backward it was kind of like finishing school.

My mom and dad still had some blow out fights. She bartended at a local country bar. One evening I woke to loud banging on my window. I wasn't sure what was happening. It was my mom. She was screaming and crying at about 2 am on a school night. I opened my window and she was screaming for me to let her in because my dad had locked her out and had her keys. I didn't understand why he had locked her out or what they were fighting about at this hour. I went to leave my room, to open the door for her and my dad was in the hallway. I don't recall what he said to me if anything. I ran to open the door. I was so embarrassed. My mom is screaming and crying in our front yard for the world to see and hear. I was sure someone in the neighborhood had heard the commotion. She came in and went into my bedroom crying. My dad walked into my room and I yelled at him. I'll never forget, I told him he was mean and I hated him. That still hits me in the gut that I said that to my dad. I hope he understood that I didn't mean it. That was a terrible night and terrible fight and an even more terrible memory.

I was a freshman at the age of 14, and I met a senior boy age 17 who liked me. I was not allowed to have a boyfriend until I was 16 years old, but I managed and snuck around. So, I started pretending I was going to school dances or events and would go out to parties. I lied about everything. I wasn't allowed to drive in a teenager's car until I was 16 years old, also. Here I was only 14 in high school and everyone was driving with friends. So, I began to lie so I could go out also. I started getting in trouble at home. I was told I had a bad attitude. I was grounded more than not.

I began sneaking out and going to parties. I started drinking at the age of 14-15. I was always lying about where I was going. I would lie about parents being present at parties. Hell, no one had parties with their parent's home! I had a big window in my bedroom that was in the front of the house. Perfect!! After my parents went to sleep my boyfriend would come and knock gently on my window and the party was about to begin. I was drinking and staying out until just before my parents would wake. I would then sleep the day away.

I became really brave and invited my boyfriend over to watch tv one evening. We didn't have a separate TV room for the kids. So awkwardly, we all sat in the living room watching tv. No one said a word. As you can imagine, he did not stay long. I told my dad that this was my house also and I should be able to have company over also. That proclamation did not go very well. I was grounded for the summer. Shortly after this, my boyfriend broke up with me. I was heartbroken, and it lasted forever it seemed. I then spent most of my time trying to be where he was. I even would get in trouble in school, so I would get detention when he had it. I thought if he saw me he would want to be with me. That was my naïve heart. I honestly believe my dad had something to do with the breakup. My dad worked on the military base and so did his dad. Enough said!! Looking back my Dad was right. That first love was going nowhere good and fast.

It was that time again, time to move. My dad had retired from the military and was taking a job in the Northeast, in Connecticut. So, he went ahead to get settled and find us a house and school. The plan was to move as soon as school ended, the end of 10th grade and I was 15 years old.

In packing, my mother came across my journal. I guess she couldn't help but to indulge herself and sat down for quite the read. As soon as she finished reading my inner most feelings she withdrew me from school. I thought she needed help packing. Not really! She sat me at the kitchen table, with my journal by her side, and asked how many times I had been drunk. Didn't know I was supposed to keep count. I knew I was in TROUBLE. I tried to play dumb, as any teenager would. She wasn't having the deer in the headlights look. Of course, she had already spoken to my dad and told him of her readings. We weren't supposed to move to Connecticut until the end of the school year, well that changed quickly. We were now moving the coming up weekend. Yes, in 3 days. Needless to say, she kept a really close eye on me. I was heartbroken. I had to leave my friends once more. I can only imagine what my sister was feeling. Unfortunately, she and I weren't that close even though we were in age.

As we drove north I felt so defeated. It was a long and terrible drive. When I saw the signs for Connecticut I felt doomed. I knew that my parents already had a psychiatrist waiting for me. I felt betrayed, not only was there a doctor waiting to see me, but my parents had my inner most secrets in hand for added ammunition. I felt like I was being punished for my feelings and thoughts.

My parents put me right into therapy at the age of 15. I was supposed to tell this strange lady everything…. I learned as a minor that I had no real privacy. My therapist and my mom would talk after every appointment. They told me it was about insurance. Sure it was. Then on every ride home, my mother would question my session. She wanted to know what I talked about. She wanted to know everything. I would lie, of course. I thought she was just nosey, that's all. Not long after starting therapy I saw a psychiatrist and was put on Prozac. I think I was high for a couple years. I can't believe my parents kept me on this drug. My brain was still developing. My parents had no knowledge of this kind of stuff. They listened to what the doctors had to say. There was no Google back then.

I entered a new High School in the middle of 10th grade. This was a whole other type of shock. I don't feel like I ever fit in very well. I had just come from the south where we wore Wrangler jeans and rode horses. In this school, I would hear kids talking about Ralph Lauren and Liz Claiborne. I thought they were students at my school. That wasn't really a funny joke. I guess I wasn't up with the times.

My first day was a mess. I met with the guidance counselor and the principal. I was given my schedule and on I went. The first class I went into was all wrong. I sat down and everyone else seemed to know I was not in the right place. A couple of students looked and my schedule and wondered why as a sophomore I was in a senior Shakespeare class. How did I get here? A teacher finally came in and reviewed my schedule and realized something was amiss. So back to the main office, I went to find out where I was supposed to be. The next class was some kind of history class. Nothing made any sense. I didn't understand what they were learning. I had learned about South Texas history and the Alamo. I had no idea what was going on. Again lost!! The next class was even better, Algebra 4. I did not understand algebra 1, let alone knowing there was a 4. I was kept in this class and failed gracefully. On to the next class, French 2. I had learned some French while in Canada and maybe one class in Texas. This class was no joke. They were only allowed to speak French in class. I was not that fluent by any means. The teacher brought me up to his desk and had me sit in the chair next to it. He put a French book in front of me and asked me to read. I thought this might not be so bad. So, I read out loud from the book he provided. He was quite surprised. He told me I had the best French accent he had ever heard. Great, but I had little comprehension of what I had read. I felt lost again. When this day finally ended I had to go find my bus. I hadn't ridden a bus to school in a long time. There were a couple of girls who were just mean. They then followed me home. My dad chased them away, but the one girl just lived down the hill. I did not have a good first day of school.

Over time I became a cheerleader. I had a very kind and loving boyfriend from a really nice family. I adjusted but still didn't really feel like I fit in. I made friends and attended school activities. I always felt like I was on the outside looking in. I became the homecoming queen, then the prom queen, and still didn't feel like I fit in.

My parents still fought a lot. When bill time of the month came they fought like crazy. Yelling at each other trying to explain why a bill didn't get paid, or where the money went. One month my mom was in charge of the bills, then my dad would be in charge the next month. Kind of back and forth went on for years. No wonder I don't know how to balance a check book. If they couldn't do it, who was going to teach me? My sister and I learned to be scarce when it was time to pay the bills.

My mom kept a clean house. I used to think it was because of my dad's military background, later found out that wasn't so true. I often said that my mom had children, so we could clean her house. Every week my mom would come up with a chore list. There was something daily for both my sister and me to do. Whatever chores were listed for the day must be completed, sometimes before school work. That was crazy to me. I thought school work should have come first. So, by the end of any week, my sister and I would have cleaned the entire house, to start a new list come Monday. She would say that she wanted the toilet to be so clean that she could eat lobster off of it. Gross! One day my chores consisted of washing and folding and putting away the towels. Not just put them away, but in a particular order to be folded specifically so they fit in the cabinet just right. Well, I messed something up because when my mom came home from work that night she woke me because the towels were not folded correctly. I reminded her I had school the next morning. She walked me into the bathroom, opened the cupboard where the towels lay folded and she proceeded to pull them all out onto the floor and told me to re-do them. It was around 1 am! I pleaded and cried but she didn't care. So, I sat there refolding the towels I had washed several hours before, with tears streaming down my face. If she wasn't "Mommy Dearest", I don't know who was.

I know my mother was diagnosed with clinical depression, but I think she also has bouts of Bipolar behavior. There would be many nights she would wake me laughing and talking really loud on the telephone. She would go through her personal phone book and call anyone and everyone. Whoever answered the phone got an ear full at 2 am. She had no sense of time or boundaries or other people's needs and schedules. She all too often was all about herself.

My junior year was particularly difficult. I was still seeing the therapist and on Prozac, but I was still depressed. All the kids at school were talking about going to college, getting scholarships, doing enough community service to get into college. This was the first I had heard about college. My parents didn't speak of college and higher education. I started asking questions, like can I go to college? Mom would always tell me I could do anything I set my mind to. Then I had to deal with my dad. I don't think he had any confidence in me. So, I went to the counselor's office and asked about college. He was so kind and very helpful. He told me what I would have to do and gave me a time frame in which things had to be done. I went home with the latest information and my dad had nothing encouraging to say. Not surprising. He thought that I should have gone to the local state college part-time and live at home. Oh, hell no!! This was my way out!! I only applied to a few schools in hopes to get into at least one of them. I don't think I had much confidence in myself. I also applied to the school that my boyfriend at the time was focusing on. Everyone said I only applied to that college because my boyfriend was going there. I denied it, but deep down it was true. My mom took me to see a few different colleges and have my interviews.

I was the first person in my family to go to college. It was a definite accomplishment. This was a way out of the house and the town I never felt right in. I have to admit that even the thought of my old high school still makes my skin crawl. It is quite possible that the issues I had with high school had more to do with me and my home life.

 Meanwhile, my depressed feelings turned into not eating. I had always been overly conscious of my appearance and size. I was thin, but always thought I could be thinner. I also tried to avoid the dinner table because many family fights began there. There was a lot of yelling in my house. This became our communication style. Whoever yelled loudest...won. It was rough. My dad's drinking had taken on a life of its own. My dad was nice when he was drinking, not so much when he was sober. Sadly, we wanted him to drink. He was nice and silly and funny and would give us money and permission to go out and anything else we could come up with. I think he might have been a bit drunk when I had him sign my college loan forms. I wanted out of the chaos and drama and depression. I often would have to wake my dad from the couch to make him go to bed. The TV was always so loud that it would wake me. I learned to use a fan to drown out the noise, I still do that today. My depression had gotten so bad that I ended up in a psychiatric unit at Yale University. I guess if I was going to crack up I might as well be at the best hospital around.

It was horrifying. During in-take, the Psychiatrist asked me questions for hours. He asked me if I had any special powers, and I told him that I could fly. That response made my mom and I to break out into laughter. The doctor did not find it as funny as we did. He gave us a puzzling look and went on. When he was done with all his questions the nurses went through my things. They confiscated things that weren't allowed like a razor or glass from a perfume bottle, a mirror, or my own medication. I entered all kinds of therapy and early in the morning. I had supervised breakfast. Group therapy, individual therapy, and more group therapy. I was missing school and a lot of it. I can only imagine what the kids at school had to say. I probably don't want to know they probably had enough of their own issues than to be concerned with me. I stayed as an impatient for a month. Then back to regular life. Only it wasn't "regular" anymore. Kids had questions and I could hear some chatting behind my back. This was so terrible in so many ways, I didn't know how to handle this kind of pressure. I started making myself throw up. I felt in control then. It lasted only a few weeks until my mom found out. Back to the doctor, we went. My mom brought me to my pediatrician, and they decided I should go back to the hospital for a short stay. When my doctor walked out of the room my mom looked at me like she was looking through me. She immediately asked "did anyone sexually abuse you? Did anyone touch you the wrong way?" I looked at her uncertain of the answer. Within moments I felt like someone had hit me up side my head and my memories came racing back to me in screenshots of the day I played on the wrong side of the fence. I told her all I could remember. I guess my mind blocked it all out until this moment. Back to the hospital, I went. Again, feeling punished for sharing my thoughts and feelings.

"The wrong side of the fence"

"Don't let people answer your destiny"

Dika Agustin

It was summer time, and I played outside like most children. We ha. blue plastic swimming pool in the back yard and I played in it all summer. Like any summer day, I had on my favorite cream-colored bikini with small flowers and ruffles. I was only 5 years old and trusting of the world around me. I didn't realize that this day I was playing on the wrong side of the fence. Charlie, the boy from across the street came to play, he was about 12 or 13 years old, like many times before. This day he brought me to the other side of our fence where there was long grass that we could hide in. There were neighbors working on their car, but they couldn't see us. He told me to be quiet. He told me he wanted me to put his penis in my mouth. I felt so gross I didn't want to do it. I remember worrying that he might pee in my mouth. He told me he wanted to put his mouth on my booby. I looked around and there was no one. He told me we had to hurry so we didn't get in trouble. He then pulled back the top of my bikini and proceeded to put his mouth on my left booby. It felt weird and yucky. Since he did that, he wanted me to put his penis in my mouth. I did. It felt so weird and dirty and yucky. Why did I have to do this? He then told me that this was a secret and we would get in trouble if we told.

Throughout this summer he came to play in my pool almost daily. I only have a few memories of the pool, but that is enough. He would swim around behind me pulling down my bikini bottoms. I would pull them back up and he would pull them down again. It went on and on, felt like an eternity. Eventually, summer was over, and my parents emptied the pool.

One day in early Autumn we had a babysitter. A bunch of kids were over to play. We were playing and climbing on a tree that was in the corner of where our yard met the one behind us. The lady whose yard was behind us had an unfriendly bulldog. She usually kept it inside if she saw we were playing outside. This day was different. Charlie happened to be in the tree as the dog ran over. The dog was barking and barking at us. Charlie slipped somehow. As he slipped the dog jumped up and grabbed his leg. All I can remember hearing was him screaming and the dog snarling. The dog was trying to pull him down. Then, what seemed out of nowhere, we heard a loud bang and the dog fell to the ground. I could see the lady just outside her back door with a gun in her hand. Everything seemed to stop except for Charlie's screams. I remember thinking I was glad he was hurt. Our babysitter ran and grabbed him and took him to his house across the street. He ended up bandaged and on crutches for a really long time. That was the last time Charlie came to my house. Later, with the babysitter, we watched out the back window as a few men came to take the dead dog away.

I blocked this out for many years. It's incredible how the mind tries to protect us. The mind continues to amaze me, even though I have a Psychology degree.

My unconscious mind tried to protect me from the trauma that had occurred. Even though I had no conscious recollection, I was exhibiting other "behavioral issues" for many years. Just because I told my mom that day what had happened didn't mean I was over it. I didn't start talking about it or healing from it until I was around 40 years of age. It's really powerful when the layers get peeled back. It is not an easy process and takes time along with a lot of courage and patience. I have had to do this in small increments. It is too big to take on all at once. However, I see my nightmares calm down and the flash backs dissipate. The memories don't go away, it's the power that they hold that goes away slowly.

"Smile and the whole world smiles with you, cry and you cry alone"

-Stanley Gordon

I heard this quote when I was a teenager. I didn't understand what it meant, yet I never forgot it.

Today, I get it!

These words hold true to so many. When you pass by someone without a smile or tears in their eyes you cannot pretend to know or understand the potential of their despair. Be careful when you stand in judgement of another. What you think to be reality may not be the same for someone else. It is possibly just smoke screens and mirrors.

For so many years I hid behind fake smiles. It was easier than explaining where the tears came from. There was a deep hole inside of me, my heart and my soul. In that hole is where all my fears, insecurities, and all the uncertainties lie. I had so many questions, and questions about questions. There was no way what I was feeling was normal. How long would this last?

What is Bi-Polar Disorder

"Live life as if everything is rigged in your favor"

Rumi

There are many facets and working pieces of bipolar disorder. Understanding these helps guide stability.

Bipolar Disorder or Manic-Depressive Disorder is a chronic mental illness that causes dramatic shifts in a person's mood, energy and the ability to think clearly. People with bipolar have highs and low moods, known as mania and depression, and mixed episodes (which is experiencing both mania and depression at the same time) which differ from the typical ups and downs most people experience. If left untreated, the symptoms usually get worse. However, with a balanced lifestyle that includes self-management and a good treatment plan, many people live well with the condition.

People with bipolar disorder have extreme and intense emotional states that occur at distinct times, called mood episodes. People with bipolar disorders generally have periods of normal mood as well.

A Manic Episode in technical terms is a period of at least one week when a person is very high spirited or irritable in an extreme way for most of the days. A person will have more energy than usual and experience at least three of the following, showing changes in behavior: exaggerated self-esteem or grandiosity; less need for sleep, talking more than usual; talking loudly and quickly; easily distracted; doing many activities at once or scheduling more into a day than can be accomplished, increased risky behavior (ie. Reckless driving, spending sprees, heightened sexual activity); and uncontrollable racing thoughts or quickly changing ideas or topics.

These behavioral changes are quite significant and are clear to those around you, especially family and friends. Symptoms can be so severe that they can cause dysfunction and problems with work, family, and friends.

Mixed State These episodes are defined by having both a manic episode and a depressive episode at the same time. This state exhibits mania with mixed features usually involving irritability, high energy, racing thoughts, rapid speech, and over activity or agitation. Depression during this episode is mixed with feelings of sadness, loss of interest in activities, low energy, feelings of guilt and worthlessness and thoughts of suicide.

NAMI (National Alliance on Mental Illness) states that in a given year, bipolar disorder affects about 5.7 million American adults and about 2.6 million of the US population 18 and older.

To diagnose bipolar disorder, a doctor may perform a physical examination, conduct an interview, and order lab tests. Though bipolar disorder cannot be identified through a blood test or body scan, tests can help rule out any other illness that can resemble the disorder, such as hyperthyroidism.

There are also physical symptoms that can give more insight when diagnosing bipolar.

Memory loss is common, especially during manic episodes. Someone may have symptoms of mania and not know what it is or even question the feelings and behaviors. The increase in energy and thinking can be fun for some, at least initially.

When I had manic episodes, before I knew what they were, I loved that time. I felt as if I could accomplish anything. I had the energy for hours and hours with no need for sleep. I have been known to jump around on my furniture and sing my heart out. Unfortunately, as I got older the mania was often mixed with depression and was a terrible feeling and all the fun was gone. I have experienced the enjoyable side of mania and really miss it. I miss the feeling of euphoria and feeling invincible. I could go on and on being so elated. I could do anything, I thought. I would go shopping and spend so much money buying such pretty things whether I needed them or not. I was enticed by the overdrive of sexual energy. There were no consequences in sight. I miss that free feeling even though I know it was a symptom of my illness that needs to be managed. Sometimes, I feel like part of me, the fun me is missing and isn't coming back.

When I do become overly energized or exuberantly talkative it is an indicator that something is just not right. These are now symptoms to be managed because they can quickly lead to a state of depression or severe agitation with relentless anger and frustration. It's a total flip from the first sign of mania to where it quickly leads.

Having shifts in energy levels can be an indicator that something is going on. Most people have normal shifts in energy throughout the day or week. A person with bipolar needs to pay attention to those energy shifts. The energy can shift between having the exuberant and excessive energy to having absolutely none and not being able to get out of bed. These extremes are very dangerous and need to be a handled swiftly and carefully. The frequency of energy shifts is just as important. If someone has bipolar with rapid cycling, their moods can quickly go up and down and back up again. These rapid cycling of moods can lead to reckless and dangerous behavior.

Clumsiness can be a symptom of mania. When mania is present the mind is overactive with racing thoughts and ideas. Everything is going fast, the mind and body. So, when trying to do things normally, while in a manic state you may have difficulty keeping up with the racing mind. You may walk into things, and trip over things or drop stuff. I can't begin to tell you how many things I have broken while I was overly energized.

Irritability can be symptomatic of depression, or a mixed state of mania. The little things become an annoyance. Aggravation comes on quickly. Things that might cause a little stress like meeting a deadline, having to keep appointments, managing home life and daily chores become more than can be handled. Irritability sets in quickly and the mood changes just as quickly.

LOST & CONFUSED   MissKellyrae's

"So many lost souls

I can now see it's not just me

Some of us are still fighting to be found

Some of us will never be found

Lost in a world of waste

How long am I willing to wait

How much more can I truely take

How many more times will I get back up when I think I've

finally given up

Is this just the beginning or is it surely the end

Is my soul really lost or was it never there at all

Am I meant to feel so broken and abused

I'm filled with sorrow and full of pain

I can't be happy because then I feel shame

Guilt eats me up and spits me back out

I'm always filled with doubt

I rather be hated then to be loved

So many things wrong with me I can't dig myself out

I keep crying out but I guess nothing really comes out

I get left with no answers"

"I don't know where I am" I cried into the phone. I had been driving around for hours in the dark with no destination. I did not know where I was or where I was going. My red mustang went so fast and my hair was blowing in the wind that flooded through the windows. The cool air felt invigorating. Uncontrollable tears fell down my face faster than I could wipe them away. My body shook as I cried and screamed.

I called my sister who lived 7 hours away. When she answered the phone all she could hear were my cries and screams. Instantly she asked me "where are you?" I tried to reply through the tears "I don't know." "I don't know where I am." "I am in my car." I think she figured that much out on her own. I remember her telling me to turn the radio down and the windows up, so she could hear me. "How long have you been driving?" she asks with fear in her voice. Again, I gave the same answer "I don't know." I had no sense of where I was and how long I had been driving around aimlessly. I heard her speaking to someone in the background telling someone that I was driving around hysterical. It was my dad!!!

My phone then beeps. I look at the screen on my phone through the tears I couldn't control, and my dad's number was called. I asked her "why is dad calling me?" She insistently told me to answer the phone. I clicked over crying even more as if that was even possible. He hears my cries and demands to know where I am. He asked "where are you? What do you see? Look around and what do see?" I replied, "I'm on a highway and I can see a McDonalds". "What highway"? he sternly asks. I meekly replied as if I was a child in trouble "91North". With such a stern voice, he demanded me to pull over and stop driving. I cried out "I can't", "I don't know". He raises his voice and threateningly tells me to pull over or he will call the police. I went into further hysterics. "No daddy, no, I can't" "You have to, now". Meanwhile, my sister is on the other line. Unbeknownst to me, she was also on the phone with my dad and able to hear my screams and cries on the phone. I just wanted the craziness in my head to stop. My thoughts were rapidly chasing around in my head with no end in sight. Even though my sister was 7 hours away she was also talking to Connecticut State Police.

My dad demands me to stop at the McDonalds I had mentioned earlier. Hell, I was already passed that. The next exit I was I got off and looped around to get back on the highway heading in the other direction. My dad demanded, "where are you now?" I replied with frustration "I turned around." My heart was pounding so hard I could feel it through my chest into my throat. My tears were falling, and they were making my skin burn. They were so sore from wiping them over and over. I still couldn't stop them from flowing.

My phone beeps, it is my sister. I guess she hung up the other phone. I told my dad that she was on the other line. He said to go ahead and answer it. I clicked over to answer her call and she blurts out "where are you?" "I turned around," I told her. "so, where are you?" "I can see McDonald's" was all I could get out. She directed me to go to the McDonalds. I had turned around again. My mind was terrified and exhausted. My body ached as it shook from the crying.

I did what she said. I turned back around and went to the McDonalds. I saw the entrance and pulled in to a parking spot. She told me to stay there that dad would be there shortly. "WHAT?" I yelled. "NO". It was only minutes until my dad arrived. I then saw all these flashing lights. I wondered "what in the hell is going on?" I hadn't realized it was all for me.

I rolled up my windows and locked the doors. I didn't want to talk to anyone. All I could do was scream and cry and pound on my steering wheel. I had no intention of talking to anyone or going anywhere with anyone. They had a different plan. There was an ambulance, 2 state troopers, my dad and his girlfriend. There was a knock on my window. I could only see bright lights. I was the state police. Great I thought. I wondered how was I going to get out of this one. He asked me to roll the window down and I screamed and cried "NO", "you are not taking me anywhere". "I am not getting out" I proclaimed. He pleaded with me to get out and I refused. He threatened to break my window and tell me the ambulance would take me. "Take me where?" I yelled, "I'm not getting out and they aren't taking me". I was still in hysterics. I was not in the state of a well minded person and that was very obvious. I truly thought in my mind that I would drive away from this and go home. My dad came to the window looking unpleased. He told me that if I didn't open the car then the ambulance was going to take me to the hospital. Somehow my dad got the state troopers to agree with him driving my car and he would take me to the hospital. Meanwhile, my sister is listening to the phone the best she could because I didn't hang up the phone earlier. Little did I know that she was the one that called the state police. That was all she could do from a distance. I think she even threatened to sue them if they didn't try to find me and take me off the road. I finally agreed to let my dad in the car. He drove me to the hospital, again.

I can only imagine the fear my sister felt. She was 7 hours away with two young children. She did what she could which was a lot being so far away. Thankfully she did what she did and was very resourceful. I sometimes wonder how that affected her. What does she carry with her, if anything? Am I still "that" sister she still worries about? Has she been able to let that deep fear in heart and soul subside? I didn't mean to scare her. I am grateful for her inner strength and laser focus to manage a crisis at a distance. Whether she realizes it or not, she saved my life that night.

My Diagnosis

"You look at me and you think I'm smiling

but I look at me and I see I'm crying"

Bridgett Devoue

I was suffering from this illness long before I received the proper care. I didn't know I had bipolar disorder. I thought I had bad PMS. I had the mood fluctuations, changes in energy, but no true idea of what I had. I sought out the help from several different healing modalities. I saw an Indian Massage Healer. The massages felt good and I was able to unveil some underlying emotional issues, but the moods still continued to swiftly change. I sought out the help of a naturopathic doctor - that didn't work. I saw a Chinese Herbalist who looked at my tongue and felt my pulse. He then made a tea concoction for me to drink. Once again, the symptoms remained and started to get worse. I had several series of Colonics to help detoxify my body. They helped with some of my constipation I was suffering from but didn't touch my moods. I even tried Urine Therapy. I didn't investigate how to use urine therapy, so I peed in a cup and refrigerated it. Then, the next morning and several other mornings I drank all I could bear. I tried this for about 2 weeks. I later found out how I was doing it all wrong. It is supposed to be diluted 100's of times. I had several different Talk Therapists. When the first therapist I saw said something I didn't like, I was on to the next one. I guess I wasn't ready to hear what they had to tell me. So, I settled with a male therapist. He was different and was referred to me by a close mentor. I often wondered if he was sleeping during our sessions. He would lean back in his brown leather chair with his eyes closed. Something was wrong or maybe I didn't understand his process. Here I am, paying $120.00 for him to sleep?? Really?? Very odd, and I didn't have a strong enough self-esteem to stop and question what was happening. Throughout our time working together he gave me a book called "An Unquiet Mind" by Kay Redfield Jamison. I cried my eyes out through the entire book. I now knew what I had been suffering with. I identified with everything the author was saying. Every emotion, up and down. The inner struggle of the mind. I knew what she meant on such a deep level. I wondered no more. In a crying fit, I called my therapist, the one who slept during our appointments, and I told him I couldn't take it anymore. He referred me to a psychiatrist.

I spent 2 ½ hours at the psychiatrist's office. He asked me question after question after question. He wanted to know the health of my family. He wanted to know about family history and if there was any mental illness in my family. They kind of seemed like random questions at the beginning. Then he began asking questions that put the nails in the coffin. I felt like all those questions were just for me. After the 2 ½ hour question interview he looked at me and said you have Bipolar I Disorder with Rapid Cycling and PTSD. He gave me a prescription and an appointment to come back in two weeks. Great, I had a diagnosis, but I had no idea what all that meant. There were abbreviations and bipolar I as opposed to II? What was the difference? So many questions with so little answers.

I had been exhibiting manic behaviors long before I knew they had a name. I had this exuberant energy that would go on for days. I felt so productive. I and my surroundings were an organized mess. In hindsight, my home space must have looked like a bomb went off. I thought I was getting things done, but now I am not quite sure what it was I was accomplishing. I could turn around at different projects, unfinished, all over the place.

 I thought I was the best in the world at what I was doing at the time, it would just take others a little while to realize my same feelings of grandeur. I could talk for hours. I would call whoever would pick up the phone. I didn't need much sleep. I felt that was a waste of time. I spent money hand over fist. If I didn't have the money I would borrow it from somewhere. I had more clothing and shoes than a person could wear in a year's time. When I was manic I had an uncontrollable desire for sex and sexual behaviors. I fed mine by working as an exotic dancer, stripper, for many years. I used this job to hide behind so much. It gave me the sexual attention I was craving. I was up all hours of the night, therefore not needing much sleep came in perfectly. I began to use the strip clubs like an ATM machine. If I got behind on a bill or wanted to take some lavish vacation, or even wanted to go on a shopping spree, I would go to work and make a ridiculous amount of money. The next day I would pay that bill, go shopping, or a lavish dinner, or a trip. When I ran out of the money back to work I went. This created a vicious cycle over time. I don't deny it was a lot of fun in the beginning. I had lots of money to take friends out, I dressed a bit more revealing. I felt like I was so much more important than the average person, grandiose.

The "FUN" of being a stripper lasted many years. Then it became something I had to do, like a chore. It still fed the crazy energy, the sexual attention, and the financial desires. As many years went through my mind and thoughts became a bit distorted. Money became my focus of everything. It didn't matter if I had a lot or had none. The desire of having money as well as not knowing how to manage it became my undoing.

I didn't have an end game. I didn't know when I would quit stripping or what else I was going to do. I had NO backup plan. I was living in the moment. I was not thinking long-term. I didn't think to save money, I figured I would do that at a later date. I thought the money would always be coming in. I didn't think there would come a time when I despised dancing. When that time crept in I was ill prepared. I was one catastrophe away from losing everything, and I did.   Money became and still is a major stressor for me to manage.

I owned a 1987 Red Ford Mustang, with a stick shift, and cream- colored leather interior. I loved that car. It was so fast and free. I drove it everywhere. I think the speed fed into my mania. If I had built up energy I would get in my car and drive, and drive, and drive. My car was the only thing I could find that could keep up with my manic energy. As the years went on, those drives often ended in crying fits. It helped release the manic energy but left nothing in its place. There were times when I would drive in such a manic state that I didn't know where I was. I still adore my fast car, but like everything else, its meaning changed.

I continue to wonder why no one explained my illness to me. All I had was a diagnosis. I knew it was bad but not as bad as it was and would come to be. I didn't know my whole life would be turned upside down. I didn't know I would lose all my relationships; friends and lovers. I didn't know I would lose my apartment in New York that I absolutely adored. I didn't know that there would come a time that I couldn't take care of myself. I didn't know that my Dad would be paying my bills and putting a roof over my head, his roof. I didn't know that I would be trying every psychiatric pharmaceutical drug to date. I didn't know I would be in and out of psychiatric units for years to come. I didn't know that I would have several different psychiatrists until I found a good one, which took about 6 years. I didn't know that I would gain 50 pounds from the medications I took. I definitely didn't know that I would endure over 23 ECT (Electroconvulsive Therapy) treatments. ECT is a procedure in which small electric currents are passed through the brain to intentionally trigger a brief seizure in hopes to quickly reverse certain mental illness symptoms such as depression. Today, I continue to have short- term memory issues. Even though I am stable for now, I have to take medication daily and will for the rest of my life. I use this as a great reminder of all I have been through and how strong I have become.

Risk Factors, Causes, and Triggers

"Say what you mean, mean what you say,

and don't say it mean"

Unknown

Causes

Unfortunately, no one knows exactly what causes bipolar disorders, aside from genetics. Studies show a strong hereditary factor, possibly due to imbalances in brain chemicals, anomalies in brain development, hormonal influences and environmental factors. Seasonal changes, lack of sleep, and childbirth may trigger manic episodes in someone who is predisposed to the illness.

In my family, there is a strong genetic influence with mental illness. Closest to me, my mother, suffers from clinical depression, and definitely has some bipolar behaviors. However, she suffers more from the depressive side of the illness. Growing up my Dad was an alcoholic. His alcoholism was a trigger as well as a contributing genetic factor. On both sides of my family, there are a lot of anxiety disorders. I also have a cousin with bipolar disorder, but he is unmedicated.

Over the years I tried to find out about mental illness in my extended family. My mother is one of eight children. My grandmother was one of 13 children and there are just about as many on my grandfather's side. I found that there was a significant mental illness in past generations. Unfortunately, many generations ago mental illness were not spoken about. This is still true today. Mental illness is pushed under the rug and not discussed. I also found that there were suicides and long term mental institutionalizations in my family. Sadly, those with mental illness back then were shamed and pushed aside without acknowledgment, to suffer alone and in silence.

Risk Factors/Limitations

One of the primary risk factors for bipolar disorder is a family history. The disorder can run in families. 80-90 percent of individuals with bipolar disorder have a relative with either depression or bipolar disorder. Some family history may consist of a parent or siblings with bipolar disorder or major depressive disorder. Other risk factors are having family members with any type of mental illness, especially ADHD, anxiety disorders, schizophrenia, or a schizoaffective disorder. Times of significant stress, a major life transition or a loss, sleep disruption and drug or alcohol abuse can also be risk factors.

Triggers

As I go through life I am deeply affected by the world around me. Sometimes it is in a positive way, and other times in a negative way. Sometimes I laugh, sometimes I get angry, other times I cry. This all sounds fairly normal. However, when dealing with a mood disorder these "normal" moods swings can get out of control and cause havoc in my life. Knowing and understanding my triggers is very important to maintaining my mental health and mental stability.

Understanding my personal limits and limitations can really help me catch an extreme mood change. However, I think the understanding comes with age, time and experience.

When I was younger I said "yes" to almost everything. I ran myself ragged not realizing there were times I should have said "no". I didn't want to disappoint anyone. I didn't really know how to stand my ground. I wanted to be accepted.

When I was diagnosed, it took many years to realize that my symptoms were years in the making. I have learned what my limits and limitations are. I have learned to say "no" which helps in my stability. There are times when I have to sit back and evaluate a situation. I have to determine if things are more than I can healthily handle. My life decisions revolve around my mental health. I am not making excuses or being difficult. What I deal with is too real to screw things up.

Sleep or the inability to sleep is a huge factor in maintaining mental health. Bipolar is an illness that does best with a well-kept routine, including sleep. I think we all know how important sleep is. The minimum recommended is a solid 8 hours. I know friends and family members who get far less and still function. I am not one of those people. I require a minimum of 9-11 hours of sleep nightly. Everyone is different. Sleep is a very sensitive thing, especially if you are not getting enough. So many things affect sleep like light, electronic devices, temperature, stress, almost anything really.

My whole life I have suffered from some type of sleep issue or another. It is now an indicator of how my mental health is doing. I can remember sitting up a 3 a.m. wondering why I was awake and the rest of the world was sleeping. Most of my life I have experienced nightmares. As I got older they really started to affect me. My nightmares are very vivid. My nightmares are in color, I feel touch, I talk and scream in my sleep. I can even smell in my nightmares. I have awoken screaming and crying not knowing what is reality and what was the nightmare. It takes a few minutes to realize that I am dreaming.

This type of disruption to my sleep can cause mania if not caught quickly. That can lead to all kinds of other problems and temporary medication adjustments, which I hate to do.

Due to my severe reactions to the lack of sleep, I always take something for sleep. I know many don't believe that this is necessary or there are other options to pharmaceuticals. This may be true and hold some validity for some. In the past, I have tried many natural approaches with no success. Disruption of sleep is too dangerous for me to play around with.

Not getting enough sleep can trigger a manic episode. A change in sleep patterns can be a symptom of bipolar disorder and also a trigger.

Nightmares are a quick indication that things are array, whether I have realized it yet or not. So, when nightmares rear their ugly heads, I have to really evaluate what is going on around me. What am I being affected by? There is often a common theme to my nightmares. I find this very frustrating. Either way, nightmares have to be dealt with, and figured out so I can get back to healthy sleep.

Through talk therapy, I have learned to de-construct my dreams and make them more understandable. With this kind of self- work, and having things in balance, I have a peaceful night's sleep with nothing to remember or haunt my day.

Alcohol & Recreational Drugs

Using alcohol and recreational drugs do not cause the illness. However, they can set off a major episode. Many people who suffer from bipolar disorder will self-medicate with drugs and/or alcohol. Before I was diagnosed I played around with the drug Ecstasy. I didn't realize I was self-medicating. There were nights, after work, that I didn't want to go home yet because I was full of energy. So, I and a friend of mine would go to an after-hours club and take Ecstasy and dance until the after the sun came up. That is not the best feeling. Walking outside, still buzzed, to get my car and go home was a really wired feeling. The sunlight was so bright, and we had been in the dark since early the evening before. It took a bit for our eyes to adjust to the brightness of the new day. I didn't want any part of the new day. I would go home and took Xanax to bring me down, so I could sleep the day away and recover from the night before. This wasn't abnormal, I thought. It was fun and felt exciting and full of thrill.

Those evenings, spent out all night, fed the manic energy I would experience. I loved the high it gave me. Adding drugs to the already manic high kept me feeling high longer. I loved feeling manic back then. I didn't experience any mixed-states or bouts of depression. I thought I was untouchable. Without knowing, I was triggering the illness that lied just below the surface.

Medications

Medications like corticosteroids, thyroid medications, and appetite suppressants can trigger a manic episode. I am unable to take any drug with a steroid, stimulants like cold medicine, or an over the counter cough suppressant. I have a very sensitive body chemistry. I am very proactive about what medications I take. I have had manic episodes be triggered by over the counter medications. Some of the drugs at the local pharmacies are very strong and should really be handled with kid gloves. We think because they don't need a prescription from a doctor, that they are safe. This is very untrue, especially when you suffer any illness, let alone one that can tear through your life like a tornado.

Seasonal Changes

Sun light is something most people take for granted. If the sun doesn't shine today than it will tomorrow. During the darker months of the year, during daylight savings, there is much less sunlight available to us. For most this is not a big deal. Those of us who suffer any type of depressive illness can really feel the effects of the light deprivation. It affects mood, eating habits, sleep patterns, and productivity.

SAD or Seasonal Affect Disorder, or winter blues, is a subset of a mood disorder in which people who have normal mental health throughout most of the year exhibit depressive symptoms at the same time every year most commonly in the winter. Due to the lack of sunlight, I notice that come January I am ready to pull my hair out and become frustrated and even aggravated. I use a therapy lamp to re-place the lack of sunlight. It's a light that I stare into in the morning for 20–30 minutes that simulates sunlight. It is very helpful during the winter months when sunshine isn't always available, and the winter blues try to sneak in.

Since I have bipolar disorder I am susceptible to severe depression in the winter months. If this occurs I have to increase my medications in hopes to prevent a long lasting deep depression that can lead to suicidal thoughts. It can be tricky to manage. While increasing antidepressants I keep in close contact with my doctor to make sure they don't bring me up too far and result in mania. The winter months are somewhat of a balancing act keeping my highs and lows in balance.

Having a Baby

Bipolar mood swings are very common after giving birth. Many women with bipolar disorder are more prone to experience bad postpartum depression, even postpartum psychosis. It can last weeks or even months. The hormonal fluctuations can trigger bipolar mania or depression. The change in sleep patterns and added or reduced medications contribute to mood changes.

Postpartum psychosis is a psychiatric emergency in which symptoms of high mood and racing thoughts, depression, severe confusion, loss of inhibition, paranoia, hallucinations, and delusions set in. They can begin suddenly with in the first two weeks after delivery. These symptoms may vary and change quickly. I am lucky to not have experienced any type of psychosis. I was told by my physician that I was at a higher risk for postpartum psychosis if I did have children.

In my early 30's I experienced two miscarriages. After the first one, I was an emotional wreck. I experienced feelings of deep depression that lead me to thoughts of suicide. I quit my job as a personal trainer over the phone. I remember walking around in circles in my apartment for hours at a time trying to pull myself together. I didn't cook or eat much at all. I did not know of my diagnosis at the time. Looking back, it explains so much. I had severe mood swings, inability to sleep well, bad temper, and I cried for weeks. I remember I was so out of control of my emotions I broke every glass and dish in my cupboard during a crazy crying fit. I was feeling so overwhelmed and saw no way out.

It took about three months until I started to feel better. I didn't seek medical help during this depression. I was in the depths of it. I didn't have another set of eyes to point out what all the disturbances in my mood were about. I didn't have much support at the time. I really felt like I was on my own, and I was. Having bipolar with rapid cycling, I can see back to where my moods went from high to low and quickly. I know the feelings of loss and severe sadness after losing a child are normal. Having bipolar these emotions go up and down with such veracity and so quickly unlike depression or sadness.

The second time I had a miscarriage, I was in a better place in my life. I was healthier overall. I had a better support system. The hormonal fluctuation, of course, affected me. I was depressed and much more moody than normal. I followed up with an OB/GYN this time. I found that support very helpful. I kind of felt relieved. I was undecided on the pregnancy and I felt like Mother Nature made the choice for me.

So many girls dream of their futures with a husband, children, home in the suburbs, and a white picket fence (maybe I am stereo-typing a bit). Point being, I was not that girl. I knew at a really young age that I was not going to have any children. I didn't want to put anyone through what I had been through. As I got older those feelings didn't change. Those feelings only grew stronger. Don't get me wrong, I love babies, toddlers, and children. It is such an impressionable and innocent time to be a part of and to witness. I've been able to experience the joy of children through my niece and nephew.

I can remember, on more than one occasion, asking my gynecologist to tie my tubes so I couldn't get pregnant. They told me I was too young, and I would probably change my mind as I get older. I did not change my mind. So, after having 2 miscarriages, I knew I was aligned with Mother Nature. I was not meant to have children of my own.

Finally, when I was almost 40 years old, my doctor agreed to tie my tubes. I felt so liberated. This was such an important decision, but I had made it years prior. After going through all I did with my illness I was so grateful that someone was actually listening to me and my reasons for not wanting children. The feeling wasn't so much not wanting my own children, but not wanting to pass this illness, that has plagued my family for years, onto another. There was a strong enough genetic link to mental illness in my family to help me make this decision hands down. I didn't want to take that chance. Who was I to make such a decision that could affect someone else so horribly? These are my feelings and beliefs. I have not regretted my decision one bit. This was the right thing for me.

Career Change/Job Loss

Feelings about job and career can affect the mood in either way- high or low. Job loss is one of the most stressful life events. The anticipation of having to find a new job or career path is extremely stressful. The financial changes that occur when changing job or career can be unpredictable. Even if a career change is wanted and planned for, it can still trigger a bipolar episode.

When I was a teenager I got my first job. I was going to be working in Carvel serving ice cream. I unexpectedly applied for the job and got it on the spot. I just happened to be downtown near the ice cream store and saw that they were hiring. I was so excited and proud of myself that I couldn't wait to get home and tell my parents. When I got home I was tickled to death and was yelling with excitement. My parents came out of their room trying to figure out what all the commotion was about. I told them "I got a job! I got a job at Carvel!" My mom was excited for me and then my dad said: "how do you think you are going to get there?" He totally deflated my excitement. I couldn't figure out why he would say that and not be supportive. My mom whispered to me "don't worry, I'll take you". That was the beginning of me realizing that my Dad had no faith in me. He didn't believe in me. That job lasted until I went to college, a couple of years. This is probably the longest amount of time that I held down a regular job.

When I went to college I had to get a job to supplement my tuition. The college counselor sent me to interview with the head football coach; he needed a secretary because the one he had was graduating. I got the job! I was pretty clueless as to what I would be doing or even how to do what he needed. Thankfully the girl I was replacing taught me a lot. So, I would work about 20 hours a week. I would go to the office after my classes or chunks of time between classes. It took me what felt like a long time to get the hang of things. Heck, I had no knowledge of football or the rules. This was my crash course to college football. It took a couple of years before I felt confident in what I was doing. I even taught myself to type during a summer break, so I could do my football job quicker and more efficiently. I was the only female in the office of a head coach, head defensive coach, and an offensive coach. There were also about 12 graduate assistant coaches. And then, of course, the football team members in and out. It kept me busy and I basically came and went as I pleased so long as the work got done. This job lasted a few years but only during school time and was only part time.

I continued to worry about doing things correctly, disappointing someone. I once had a job at a bank. I passed the class but still was not confident in what I was doing. I felt on the spot every time a customer came to my window. I always needed help. Some of the customers would say "oh, you are new" and not in a nice way. My drawer was never right at the end of the day. I was always off by a few cents. I was told that if my drawer was off more than three times I would be let go.

I was going through some medication changes again. Getting up at such an early time was terrible. I don't think my medication from the night before had enough time to wear off. I would be at the bank, but I would be drifting off. I couldn't keep my eyes open. It was awful and embarrassing. I really was trying. Then I had to be hospitalized again and was absent from my job. I didn't want to tell them what was going on. After being hospitalized my Dad brought me to my sister's in Maryland because there was no one to "take care" of me. I was able to keep the bank job for a little while, however, they insisted on knowing what was going on or what I had. I was in no way prepared to fight for my job. I let it go and never returned their phone calls again. It was more than I could handle. I felt a bit deflated and unsure if I would ever be able to hold down a job.

I have yet been able to hold down a "normal" job, though I have tried many times unsuccessfully.

Relationships and Intimacy

"The most painful truth is I loved you and the most beautiful lie is you loved me too."

Suri Singh

Relationships and intimacy are important for normal health. They can be especially trying when you have a mental illness. I know it is hard to keep up with relationships while you feel unbalanced. Unfortunately, many people don't understand the moods or what you are going through. Many relationships don't survive this illness, and many families are destroyed. The significant other in a relationship may wonder how long do they hold on to their relationship? Will things change and get better? Will the intimacy return? When will we have sex again? When should they walk away to save their own sanity?

Many diagnosed with bipolar disorder may have experienced a wild sex life. Overtly sexual feelings and behaviors are a symptom of the illness. You may have even been sexually reckless. It is all part of it. So, if your partner was with you prior to your diagnosis they have probably experienced a great sex life with you. Once you start a medication protocol your sex life may suffer. There are many side effects of psychiatric medication and loss of sex drive is one of them. It almost feels like a bad punishment. You probably experienced your intimacy in relationships through sex though they are two different things. That might be the only way you have experienced intimacy since you possibly thrived with sex. Your partner might mistakenly take the side effects of the medication to you creating distance between the two of you or feeling rejected and angry. You may not notice the physical distance due to everything else you are dealing with.

Intimacy is a feeling of closeness, affection, togetherness, and having warm feelings toward another. It is a beautiful thing when experienced between two people openly and lovingly. Since psychiatric medication has a slew of symptoms and it is easy to fall prey to them. Unfortunately, loss of sex drive, inability to reach climax, and for a man, the inability to maintain an erection are all side effects and can be devastating.

When the person with bipolar is in the throes of a manic or depressive episode they are not able to relate to others very well. Bipolar disorder brings on a multitude of issues. You can follow all your protocols like medication compliance, self-monitoring of moods, keeping a mood journal, keeping your scheduled doctor appointments, and therapy sessions and still suffer from some type of unbalance or relapse.

Every relationship is different, there are no two the same. What might destroy one relationship; another may deepen their desire to succeed through the difficult ups and downs. The relationships that survive or even thrive have deep insight, they have reasonable expectations of each other and their relationship, and do not get lost in denial or distance. Both people in the relationship must bring their best selves and intentions to the relationship. The one with the illness must be motivated by their treatment plan and maintaining health. The partner must bring understanding, forgiveness, emotional maturity, and a ton of patience. They must have an understanding of the illness or be willing to learn about what they are up against. It is a complex illness.

Due to the sexual side effects, you must learn how to have intimacy in your relationship in ways other than sex. You can experience intimacy by hugging, kissing, holding hands, snuggling, taking walks together, having a conversation, reading to one another, taking a drive and singing to the music. There are a lot of ways to be intimate with your significant other you just have to be willing to put in the work and time it takes to build and re-build your closeness.

Before I was diagnosed I had many different sexual partners over the years. I am over the embarrassment of my behaviors from my illness. Looking back, I can see some of the major life decisions I made while in a manic state, unbeknownst to those around me.

I was married when I was much younger. I rushed us into and rushed us out of it. He was a wonderful friend to me and a loving husband. I can see how my undiagnosed illness played havoc on that relationship and those to come. I knew I was in no place and completely unable to give him the kind of love he deserved. He came from a very supportive and loving family. I envied that in a way. After the relationship ended I wondered if I had made the wrong decision or made the decision without thinking. He now has a loving marriage and beautiful children he so deserved. I am truly happy for them.

When I left my first marriage I moved to a small town just outside of Manhattan, NY. I moved to NY with dreams of becoming an actress. I attended weekly acting classes. I went on auditions and even booked a few small parts. I fell in love with New York. It felt freeing in a way.

I had many boyfriends and some at the same time. I craved sex as a way to feel close to someone. That did not last very long. If the sex was wild I continued until I got bored. Some of them I cared for, others it was pure sex. I did fall for a man that I really cared for. I think he was a bit too sensitive to handle the throes of the illness. This relationship existed prior to my diagnosis, and through the very first parts after the diagnosis and medications. I have to admit that I was all over the place. I was with him and broke it off and on and back again. He was hoping that the doctors would "fix" me so he and I could be better. I remember calling and calling him with no return call. He reached a point where he had to protect himself and his feelings. In the throes of it for me, I felt a bit abandoned when he went across the country to take a temporary job. I had nothing in me to try and make that relationship work; it just wasn't meant to be. I can see how difficult it can be for the other person in a bipolar relationship. I don't have any ill feelings toward him or the lost relationship. I honestly don't believe that I would have wanted to be in a relationship with me at that time. Any type of relationship can be affected by this illness. Even my girlfriends backed away, or I pushed them away. I had nothing to give to myself let alone to someone else.

Now that I am in a healthy relationship I see all it entails. From him, it truly takes a lot of patience and understanding. I appreciate all he does for me. He is able to tell when I have a hair out of place. He can see behavior changes long before I recognize them. There are tell- tale signs for me when things are beginning to go array. He will step in and let me know what he sees and usually what is causing the upset. He has really taken the time to be my friend, understand my illness, and love me unconditionally. Sometimes there are bumps in the road, but we get through them. I have a great team around me that helps my mental illness not take over my life. It is an illness that I have, not an illness I am.

If you are lucky to have one or two people on your side and there for you, do your best to hold on to them. When I got sick I lost all the friends I had at the time. 13 years later, I have contact with maybe three of the friends I once had. Relationships are difficult because they are give and take. There are many times when you are unable to give. Do your best to hold on to the real and healthy relationships you do have. I have found that I have isolated myself so much that when I look around I only have a couple of friends. Pushing myself out the door to meet new people has been almost impossible. I often find that I want girlfriends, but I have lost some of the skills to do so. This is something I know is an issue for me and one that I really need to work on. I must admit that I have envy in the way that my sister is able to make friends no matter where she lives. She has lived all over and abroad and somehow ends up having several girlfriends in no time at all, and they are good people. I rationalize it in my head by thinking it is because she has children. Many women make friends through "mommy groups". I am not a mommy so that avenue isn't available to me. I will have to dig deeper and make more efforts, even if they are out of my comfort zone. Through all this I learned I am more of an introvert than an extrovert. Trying to push myself to be out-going has never worked well or felt good.

Suicide & Shame

"Though the course may change
sometimes, the river always reaches the sea"

Unknown

Reaching any type of stability was a long time coming. I was and am still very sensitive to chemical changes. Within the first couple months on medication, I gained weight rapidly. I caught that in the bud quickly. As a result, a medication change. So, between not wanting to strip anymore, not knowing how I would take care of myself financially, and along with a medication change I was a walking suicide poster. I was traveling from NY to Massachusetts to "work". It was a 2- hour drive. This was a lot of time for my mind to go in circles around itself. One day, in particular, I had no money and had received an eviction notice on my apartment and had changed a medication. With all this baggage weighing on my shoulders I drove toward work. I cried the whole way. The feelings I was having were all over the place. I remember my focus being on work and having to go because I needed the money to keep a roof over my head. I didn't know how long I could continue this. I had just turned 30 and I had no money, no savings, no future plan. I was having trouble figuring out what I should do. By now I had driven up and down the same highway a few times. Back and forth like a magnetic pull. I went over the same bridge several times and thought driving my car off the bridge would be an end to all this craziness my mind didn't have control over. I was scared and all alone. I wasn't even sure where I was, just on a highway. I drove around for about 4 hours, obviously late for work. I couldn't contain the tears and the screams that accompanied them.

I finally called my mom with a question. I only wanted an answer, not everything that I got. I asked her if I went to the hospital how long would they keep me? I couldn't stay long, I needed to work, but I couldn't function like this, and I was coming upon the bridge again. She told me I needed to go to the hospital. Not what I wanted to hear but looking back the only realistic option. She asked me where I was and all I could tell her was that I was in my car somewhere in Connecticut. She said to call my dad. He was the closest person to me physically. I hung up the phone in defeat. I phoned my dad and told him I thought I needed to go to the hospital but didn't know where to go. Famous question, he asked me where I was. The famous answer, I don't know. He went on to ask me what I saw and what was around me. I told him I just crossed the Sikorsky bridge. He reminded me that he lived only two exits away and asked if I remembered how to get to his house. I said yes, and he told me to meet him there, now!

That drive sucked. All I could think about was having to go into a hospital, again. Since the high school hospitalization was a flop, I could only wonder what would happen this time. I met my dad, locked up my car, and got into his truck. I proceeded to take off any jewelry I had on knowing the hospital would take it. My dad decided to take me to St.Raphael's Hospital. I refused to speak to the first nurse at the ER. My dad told her something about me being suicidal and a psych nurse quickly took me in the back. This wasn't the normal place you go when you go to the ER, that was obvious when the door locked behind me. This was for real.

In this room, there were several other patients blocked from one another only by a curtain. I don't think I had quit crying yet. Someone came in and handed me hospital clothing to change into. I refused several times, only to cry in hysterics. The nurse finally told me that if I didn't change my clothes that they would do it for me. I think I cried even harder. In no way was I going to let them change my clothes, so I gave in and changed. Nurses and doctors came and went with an occasional question. They were not sure what to do with me since I was living in NY and had a Psychiatrist there that was treating me. The ER doctors finally were able to contact him.

I was then brought into a real room with the door closed. It was the hospital psychiatrist and someone else, probably an intern. He proceeded to ask me questions. First, he wanted to know how I got there. What happened in my day that I ended up there, in that room, at that time. He asked other questions. He asked about my sexual partners and I told him I didn't know I was supposed to keep count. He then went on to ask if I knew I could contract an STD. Like that was my concern at that point. I remember he asked me what day it was, but I didn't know the date. I couldn't figure out why he was asking me what seemed to be trivial questions. He asked if I knew who the president was, how many miles is it to California. He might as well have been asking me about monkeys. I was hoping this wasn't a test because I surely failed.

He told me I was in a mixed manic state. Great, what did that mean I wondered. It meant I was staying. They returned me to my curtain enclosed cubical where my dad awaited. The doctors and nurses came in and started asking about my financial situation. They wanted to know if I had a savings account, yeah right. They wanted to know if I had any mutual funds, yeah right. They asked if I had any type of insurance, nope. It was kind of embarrassing having my dad hear about my lack of financials. I was there for several hours while they found a bed for me at another hospital inpatient facility in Middletown CT. An ambulance arrived, and they took me away. It was late, and I was so tired. I guess I was coming down from my mixed manic state. This was the beginning of what became my many inpatient hospitalizations.

Suicide is the taking of one's own life.

Shame is a painful emotion caused by the belief that one is, or is perceived by others to be, inferior or unworthy of affection or respect because of one's actions, thoughts, circumstances, or experiences.

Bipolar disorder can cause many to experience shame. Since this is a mood disorder, the moods change, sometimes without warning. Often, our moods dictate our behavior. There are times when someone is experiencing mania and do all kinds of crazy things that they would not normally do if their mood was stable. Then when the mania is gone, they look back or are told of their erratic behaviors. Sometimes they don't remember them at all. Over time this adds up. The recollection of "bad" behaviors can lay heavily on one's mind and create feelings of embarrassment or shame. This illness is an all-consuming challenge requiring a lot of stamina and even more courage. Not only do we have to deal with our own unrealistic ideas and thoughts, we have to manage our outward behaviors. It's the unexplained actions, mood swings, and behaviors that cause others to look at us with wonder.

What do you do, where do you go, who do you contact when you feel like your whole life has fallen out from under you? Most people will reach out to a friend or family member for some advice or an empathetic ear. Some will take a walk to their favorite park or beach to clear their minds or organize their thoughts with a journal or possibly music in hand. Others will go online to rant their difficulties. These are all great ideas if you think of them during a trying time.

Unfortunately, those who suffer from suicidal thoughts do not feel like there is anywhere or anyone to turn to. In the darkest moment, right before a suicide attempt, there is nothing. Life feels completely empty, the mind, body, and soul. Ending life seems to be the only way to end the pain of emptiness.

When someone we know or hear of has committed suicide, we ask why? Why seems to be one of the first questions. Others don't understand but want to. When we see celebrities commit suicide we don't understand because society thinks that they have it all. Having a life of privilege, or financial wealth, or even success doesn't keep you safe from the depths of depression that can lead to suicide. Suicide doesn't judge, and you can't tell that someone is suicidal by looking at them. It's a quiet and desperate place.

How does one end up in that empty place? There are so many different roads to the feelings of suicide. There are feelings of hopelessness, no self- worth, a stagnant emptiness. There may be an acceptance of the end, in that moment. The feeling of connectedness to others has dissipated. The feelings of self-worth have no meaning if they exist at all.

I have had suicidal thoughts, with plans in place, more times than I can remember.

My first attempt was when I was around the age of 14. At that time, I felt like I was irrelevant. I didn't think I mattered to anyone. My mom was out of town helping my brother deal with his issues of addiction. My boyfriend, that I wasn't allowed to have, had recently broken up with me. My dad was over my "bad attitude" and I was grounded, once again. I was in my bedroom. I didn't want to live anymore, and I didn't think anyone cared. I got a bottle of Motrin from my mom's medicine cabinet and went into my room. I remember it was sunny in mid- afternoon, on a Saturday. It was during what I call the lull of the day. The bottle was ¾'s full. I took a handful, then some more. I went to lay in my bed hoping I would quietly pass away in my sleep. I figured my dad would find me at some point. Several hours later I woke up. Imagine my surprise that I was still alive. I didn't know what to do next considering I didn't plan on being here. I went on with the day feeling horrible, physically and emotionally. I still had the feelings of suicide, but I didn't have a second plan. So, I suffered in my mind in silence. I didn't tell anyone but my journal.

Treatments

"How beautiful you bloom when you nurture your roots"

gemmatroy

When it comes to treating a mental illness, pharmaceutical drugs are the doctor's first treatment usually started. Drugs are started and quickly and often during some type of crisis. For some, it's a life saver. Antidepressants can help a person out of a deep, suicidal depression. Mood stabilizers can bring someone down from a dangerous manic high. There are times when doctors have to give drugs to level things out to then figure out what is really happening. When a person is in an extreme mental state, talking may not do much. Doctors are treating symptoms, not the underlying issues at this point.

I have had personal experience in being treated with medication and then figuring out the rest later. As needed as this way of treatment is, it carries its own difficulties. Once on psychiatric drugs, it can be difficult to get off them and that can create a vicious cycle.

Pharmaceutical Drugs

Drugs have an intended effect on the body. In the process of helping, they can sometimes put the body in a dangerous state by slowly depleting the nutrients needed to maintain health and to help heal.

I have found how overmedicating can have an extreme effect on my life. Controlling the chemicals in my body is a critical part of staying healthy with bipolar.

Today there are so many different psychiatric drugs that it is hard to keep count. I, personally have been on and off over 33 different Psychiatric Medications in total. Most changes came with terrible complications. Each doctor has their own "go to" drugs they prescribe. In my health history, I have had several different prescribing physicians. Looking back, it seems that every new physician I had, they had their own "go to" drugs that they would switch me to. It was often inconsistent, and unorganized. It seemed that the newest doctor didn't care whether I was doing well on the current medications or not.

There was a time when I had to attend an outpatient program. With this program, I was assigned a therapist and a prescribing physician. I say, "prescribing physician" because I didn't always have a regular psychiatrist. As I got comfortable with one doctor, another would arrive in his place. I was once switched to a new female psychiatrist and she was horrible! When I went into her office she seemed out of her depths. She looked and seemed totally confused. She told me not to speak, only answer her questions. I couldn't figure how this was going to work. I had been on a sleeping pill for several years. I am not sure her reasoning, but she took me off the sleeping pill and gave me Benadryl. Needless to mention I did not sleep which led to a mixed manic state and back into the hospital I went. I don't think some doctors grasp the magnitude of events that can transpire by their aloofness and inability to see the extreme impact that pharmaceuticals have on bipolar patients. I have no idea what some of these prescribing physicians are thinking. Unfortunately, those of us with the illness suffer from their "mishaps". This is not conducive to good mental health. I would NOT recommend this type of care to anyone.

Drugs are labeled into categories for what illnesses or symptoms they treat. Some drugs are used for what's called "off-label" reasons. This means that a drug may be used for its side effects instead of what it is originally made for. For example, many drugs cause drowsiness, therefore they could be used to help sleep even though it's designed to treat other symptoms. I presently take Seroquel with success for mood stabilization. It is also used to help with sleep. There are times when I am over stressed or overwhelmed by something happening in my life and my mind gets busy with nothing, that's what I call it. It's the beginning of mania creeping in. When this begins it is usually detected by those around me first. I'm just stuck in my head. When these feelings occur, I can take a little extra of my medication to quiet my mind down. It works wonderfully, however, I forget I have the relief sometimes. My mind gets so fast and busy that I forget there is help on the shelf.

Since doctors do use medications for off label reasons you have to be diligent and present in your own health care. It is so important for your health to know what drugs you are on and at what dosage. You need to know why a particular drug was prescribed so you know if it is having the intended effect or not. You need to know what the drug is supposed to do for you. Take an active role in your medication management. You may need to keep a journal. I find at times when I have had to add a dosage that writing it down helps me remember if I took it or not. I have found over the years that some doctors are over-sensitive to my questions. Maybe they think we are questioning their abilities. It is a fine line sometimes. I think that all the practitioners in a health team should work together to ultimately help in finding some type of stability. Neither of my doctors wants to agree that my constipation is due to my medication. I realized I needed to figure it out on my own. I have a magnesium deficiency therefore, I supplement daily with a magnesium blend of 3 different types of magnesium to avoid constipation. Since I have been doing this I have been quite regular. I know talking about bowel movements is not a sexy topic. My friends, having an illness is not sexy. I nourish what's out of balance in order survive on a daily basis.

Even though these drugs are prescribed to help existing symptoms, they can also drain the body of important nutrients and minerals. I am not a doctor however, I believe in supplementation. I have always taken an array of vitamins and minerals to aid my body while taking medications. Unfortunately, our foods are not what they use to be. Today, due to pesticides and over farming of our fields, our foods lack in the nutrients they once had, and we depended on.

Being on psychiatric medications can come with a lot of side effects. Some are life threatening some are mild and others are only a daily nuisance. Constipation is one of the common side effects that I suffer from.

It took me about 5 years, several different doctors, many hospitalizations, a lot of different therapists, intolerable group meetings, desires of suicide, weight gain, no social life, a family at its wit's end, and only then did I start to develop some stability in my life. Not everyone will have this chaos. Some may have less, others more. You can't give up. We all must keep trying.

There are many commonly used psychiatric medications. Many drugs are used for an array of symptoms or illness and can feel like a wild roller coaster ride if not taken carefully.

Drugs that are used for anxiety or panic disorders are called Benzodiazepines (Benzos). Benzos are habit forming and can lead to dependence. They have side effects such as lightheadedness, drowsiness, confusion, sedation, memory impairment, improper body balance, fatigue, constipation, weight gain, dry mouth, and reduced libido. You may experience only a couple of these side effects or none at all. Make sure you let your prescribing physician know of any and all side effects that you experience.

Benzos are known for depleting B Vitamins, B-1, Biotin, Calcium, Vitamin D, and K, and good intestinal bacteria.

Aside from eating a nutritious diet on a regular basis, I would and do supplement with a good Multi Vitamin/Mineral, I also add a complete vitamin B100. Since we don't get enough Vitamin D from the sun I also supplement with Vitamin D. And most importantly, I use a probiotic to put the healthy bacteria back into my gut.

Drugs that are used for depression are called antidepressants. Some of the common side effects consist of dry mouth, diarrhea, constipation, sleep problems, change in weight, sexual disturbances, change in appetite, headache, and drowsiness. Again, make sure you let your prescribing physician know of any and all side effects that you experience. Importantly to know that this family of drugs are not good for someone with bipolar disorder. They can cause mania.

Antidepressants are known for depleting B Vitamins, Omega 3s, Vitamin D, Glutathione, Calcium, Vitamin k, Vitamin C, Melatonin, CoQ10, Folate, and minerals such as Zinc, Selenium, and Manganese.

Again, a nutritious diet on a regular basis will help as a foundation for your bodies overall health. I then supplement with a Multi Vitamin/Mineral, also a complete B100. I also take a balanced Omega, which is your healthy fish oil. The Omega 3 and 6 need to be balanced properly, be sure to look for that. I add a Glutathione for my brain health.

ADD/ADHD or attention-deficit/hyperactivity disorder is treated with stimulants. Some of the common side effects consist of decreased appetite, stomach pains, and sleep problems. Again, those with bipolar disorder have to be cautious with stimulants, they can cause mania. I experienced a manic episode while taking medication for attention deficit disorder. I was not able to take a dosage high enough to help the disorder. It was very frustrating. I was positively hoping it would work for me in that I was having a lot of trouble focusing. I had to discontinue the medication because playing around with mania is too risky.

Stimulants are known for depleting B Vitamins, Vitamin C, and Potassium.

A well- balanced diet will aid in the overall health of your mind and body. With these experienced depletions, be sure to integrate good sources of vitamin C like citrus fruits, and bananas for the added potassium, I would again and always add a Multi Vitamin/Mineral, a complete vitamin B100.

Mood-Stabilizing Medications are used for bipolar disorder and schizophrenia. These drugs help balance certain brain chemicals that control emotional states and behaviors. They can help to treat the mania and prevent the return of both manic and depressive episodes in bipolar disorder and the depression in schizophrenia. Most common side effects consist of nausea, diarrhea, increased thirst and increased need to urinate, weight gain, drowsiness and trembling.

It is important to know that your physician often thinks that the benefits out way the side effects. Be sure to discuss any side affects you might experience with your physician.

Mood Stabilizers have been known to deplete your body of B Vitamin, folate, Vitamin D, Biotin, Calcium and Vitamin K.

Again, a well-balanced diet is a great starting point for gaining and maintaining mental health. I also supplement with a well-balanced Multi Vitamin/Mineral, a B100, and vitamin D since it is almost impossible to get the amount you need from the sun.

Antipsychotics, also known as major tranquilizers and are a class of medications used to treat psychosis, schizophrenia, and bipolar disorder. They treat symptoms of delusions, hallucinations, paranoia, and confused thoughts. There are two classes of antipsychotics called typical and atypical. Typical Antipsychotic drugs were first developed in the 1950's and were used to treat psychosis. They may also have been used to treat acute mania and agitation. Atypical Antipsychotics are a group of drugs which can have severe side effects, they are thought to be safer than the typical antipsychotics. I have taken several of these drugs but the side effects too much for me to bare.

Side effects of the following could be drowsiness, sedation, nightmares, amnesia, constipation, weight gain, dry mouth, heart burn, tardive dyskinesia (unwanted movement).

Since these drugs can cause cravings for complex carbohydrates, you have to be aware of this when making choice around food consumption. Having these types of cravings can cause weight gain. You have to carefully choose a healthy diet full of unprocessed foods, fresh fruits, and vegetables. Be careful on the carbohydrates you choose. I also supplement with a balanced Multi Vitamin/Mineral, vitamins B100, and an additional Folic acid, especially if you are wanting to get pregnant.

I have been on many medications that treated my bipolar very well. Sadly, the side effects were too bad to continue with the drug. For example, I was on Abilify, and it worked really well. Unfortunately, I started to have twitching in my fingers, therefore I was taken off of that and onto another drug. I was put on a drug called Invega. Again, this drug worked really well however, I began lactating, so I have to come off this drug. I was then put onto Cymbalta. This drug worked really well again, then I started to twitch in my fingers and had to come off that drug. This is the roller coaster of medication.   The trial and error of attaining stability.

Psychoeducation is and can be so helpful. I and my family did not receive any, but I wish we did in hindsight. It helps the patient and families to have a better understanding of the illness. It helps in addressing the stigmatization of mental health concerns and mental health awareness. The goal of psychoeducation is to help people to better understand and become accustomed to living with mental health conditions is the main aspect of all therapies. Generally, it is known that those who have a thorough understanding of the challenges they are facing as well as the knowledge of personal coping ability, internal and external resources, and their own areas of strength are often better able to address difficulties, feel more in control of the condition and have a greater internal capacity to work toward mental and emotional well-being.

Psychoeducation leads to increased compliance with treatment regimens. When people who have been diagnosed with a mental health condition are able to understand what the diagnosis means, they are more likely to view their illness as a treatable condition rather than a shameful diagnosis indicating they are "crazy".

Talk therapy is a very useful therapy to have at some point in time. Therapists that do talk therapy can vary in their title and experience. Some are Social Workers with a private practice, others have a Ph.D. in psychology or social work or they are marriage and family therapists. There are a variety of "therapists".

Talk therapy is kind of like the movies, you sit in one chair or couch and they sit across from you for your conversation. Therapists can help you find the root issue of what is going on at the time.

I have seen several different therapists over the years dating back to high school. Some, have been very helpful, others not so much. Sometimes I would fire them because I didn't like something they said. I recall vividly doing that at least twice. One therapist, I had was very good until she asked me when I was going to grow up? I didn't like that question at the time, fired! I also fired my very first therapist. I didn't choose her, my parents did. When I was in an inpatient hospital during high school my therapist came to visit me. She had a student therapist along with her for teaching purposes. That day was particularly difficult. I was on a lot of Prozac, probably more than I should have been. I was very reactive to almost anything. Prior to her visit, I had been in a group therapy with about 25 other patients. It was terrible. It was a really big room, and no one could hear what others had to say. It lasted for about an hour. I was aggravated, probably due to the high dose of Prozac. By the time she arrived it was late in the day and I wanted nothing to do with her. I remember my head felt like it was spinning and was really fast and hurt badly from the inside. I know now that I was in the midst of a mixed manic state. She didn't get many words out when I yelled at her. She was fired, and I never wanted to see her again. That was that. Overall, I have found talk therapy to be quite beneficial. I have been able to figure out what my triggers for mania and depression are. I have learned to set boundaries in my relationships. I have learned to stand up for myself. I have learned to deconstruct my nightmares when they rear their ugly heads. I have even learned that it is ok for me to lean on my medications when I need to.

ECT (Electroconvulsive Therapy)

"Losing Control

The world around me is cloudy

And the thoughts in my mind are unclear

I'm reaching the end of my patience

And I'm starting to relive my fear

I'm losing control of my life

That's a scary thing to say

The world that I knew before me

Is slowly slipping away

The friends that I had are gone

It's shocking because it's true

And once again I'm alone

And I don't know what to do

The trust that I had for life

Is slowly dissolving with time

I've lost my sense of reality

I no longer believe what I see

Sometimes when I stand in front of the mirror

The reflection starring back isn't me

I'm losing control of myself

I'm losing control of my mind

The only thing that I have left

Is the patience and abundance of time"   by Edith SaintFelix

The following chapter contains graphic descriptions of Electroconvulsive Therapy.

Electroconvulsive Therapy (ECT) is a procedure that is still done today. It is used to cause changes in the brains electrical workup that can quickly reverse symptoms of certain mental illnesses, especially depression. ECT is done under general anesthesia, in which small electric currents are passed through the brain, intentionally triggering a brief seizure.

The procedure takes about five to 10 minutes and that includes time for preparation and recovery. It can be done while an inpatient at a hospital, or as an outpatient procedure.

ECT is used to treat: Severe depression, treatment-resistant depression, severe mania, catatonia, and agitation and aggression in people with dementia. It may be a good treatment option when medications are not tolerated, or other forms of therapy haven't worked.

Even though ECT is considered generally safe, risks and side effect may include confusion, memory loss, nausea, headache, jaw pain, or muscle aches.

Personally, I have undergone in upwards of 20+ ECT treatments. At the time, medications were not working. I was experiencing severe side effects from pharmaceuticals which kept landing me in an inpatient hospital setting. This was the final thing that doctors said I could try. I was desperate. I don't think I had a full comprehension of what was about to take place. I was transferred from one hospital to another that did ECT treatments. I spent a month in that hospital undergoing ECT treatments, three times a week.

The first morning, early a nurse came with a wheelchair to take me to my ECT treatment. I was unable to eat breakfast because I was going to be under anesthesia. The nurse wheeled me out of the locked doors and into the elevator. We went to the first- floor surgical recovery room. I didn't understand why I was going into surgical recovery since I didn't and wasn't having surgery. As soon as the door opened I could feel a chill in the air it was really cold. There was a medical cart full of pastries. They looked so good, especially since I didn't eat breakfast. A nurse greeted me and introduced herself. She gave me a hospital gown to put on, but I could keep my panties on. Once I was dressed she showed me to a hospital bed that I was to get into. It was one of four beds that were lined up against the far wall of the surgical recovery room. Each bed was separated only by curtains. I was so cold I asked for an extra blanket. The nurse brought me over a nice warm one. There was a lot of shuffling around. There were three nurses in this post-operative recovery room. My doctor walked in and asked if I was ok. I must have looked scared to death because I was. He explained briefly how the process would take place. There would be an anesthesiologist who would check on me shortly. He went on to explain that there would be a blood pressure cuff on my arm to monitor my blood pressure. There would also be one on my lower leg, but I wouldn't know it was there because it would be used while I was under anesthesia. I found out later that the cuff on my leg helped them figure out when I was in a seizure. The doctor would put a gel on my temples and place two separate round electrical conductors, they looked like cymbals, the musical instrument. Once I was unconscious the doctor hooked everything up, created the seizure that would last only seconds. Then everything would be removed, and the recovery nurse would wake me. The procedure itself only takes about 5-10 minutes from beginning to end.

I got familiar with the process since I was having them three times a week. Each time was a little different. I learned to ask for what I wanted. I had seen a few different anesthesiologists. One was so easy going and would give you whatever you wanted to make you feel more relaxed. I liked him. When the anesthesia is administered it burns the veins going in. I could watch the doctor hook up a syringe full of a white solution (that was the actual anesthesia), I followed it as it went into my IV that was connected to the top of my hand. Then I felt the burning. I could feel the burning in my hand and then up my arm to about my shoulder and I was out! I learned later that I could have a numbing agent put into my IV just prior to the anesthesia and there would not be any burning feeling. That was a great lesson to learn. Even now, if I have a procedure I know to ask for the lidocaine prior to anesthesia.

I remember being told that if I did the ECT treatments I would no longer need to take pharmaceutical drugs. Well, I still take medication even though I underwent the ECT treatments. I feel like I was misled a bit. It became a really stressful and intense time. My family was overwhelmed. While I was inpatient going through ECT I was alone. My dad would come visit in the evenings when his schedule allowed. I had no other family around for support. My friend, that became my true love would visit a few days a week. My family, most being at a geographical distance wondered if this final grasp at straws would work.

Since I was in-patient when I started the ECT, I got into a pattern. I knew what to expect. I knew who the nurses were, and they knew me by name. They knew that after I woke I wanted apple juice and a blueberry muffin. After having anesthesia, the nurses required that I eat and drink something before I could be discharged. Once I was awake and alert the surgical nurse would call up to the hospital floor I was on to request that someone come and get me. Soon after a nurse would arrive with a wheelchair and back up to the locked unit and into bed, I went. I would sleep most of the day. When I did finally wake I suffered painful headaches and jaw pain. I was told that was normal. This continued every Monday, Wednesday, and Friday for a month. I was also having medications changed during this time.

Once I was discharged from the hospital, I continued to have the ECT on an outpatient basis. They continued to be three times a week. At first, my dad would bring me to my treatments. He could only bring me for a few weeks because he had a job and couldn't miss all this time. He tried. He did the best he could with the situation at hand. I can only imagine what that time was like for him. He is the kind of man that likes to "fix" things. He couldn't fix me this time. All he could do was watch and probably pray that this would work. Since he was unable to take me his girlfriend at the time took me to several treatments. Again, she could only uproot her life for so long. She tried, and I am grateful for that. Since I didn't have anyone else to take me, the doctors arranged for me to be picked up and dropped off by a medical car service.

Upon my arrival as an outpatient, I had to sign an authorization form for the treatment. I don't recall signing these forms, but I must have. I could have been signing my life away for all I knew. My memory was compromised due to the treatments. I don't think I was in any state to be signing any type of authorization. I was able to review most of my medical records and saw that I was not the one who signed most of the forms, one of the doctors did.

When I was inpatient I was always in the first of the four hospital beds. Occasionally I would see another gentleman in the next bed. We were only separated by a curtain. I could hear him, and he could hear me. When I was having my treatments on an outpatient basis I was no longer in the first bed. I would be in the second bed and even sometimes the third. That meant that the patients in the first two beds would have their ECT before me. This became a bit traumatizing. I could hear the entire procedure happening for whoever was in the first bed, and then again for the second bed. I was so anxious by the time they got to me. My heart felt like it was coming out of my chest. Once I was hooked up to the monitors my doctor noticed how overwhelmed I was feeling by my heart rate and blood pressure. I remember one morning I was in the third bed. Not happily. I was thinking maybe if I could only get there earlier this would all be different. On this particular morning, there was a female in the first bed. Great I thought but little did I know. There was a lot of shuffling around this morning. I couldn't see what was happening, I could only hear since we were only separated by a thin curtain. Terrible setup. As they prepped the girl in the first bed I could hear the fear in her voice. They told her they were putting in her IV. Shortly after they had her IV in I could hear the anesthesiologist tell her that she would be falling asleep soon. They asked her to count to 10. She started crying out, but I couldn't understand her words. I could hear the nurses comforting her and reassuring her that she would be fine. Hearing her struggle while going under anesthesia was quite disturbing. I know it's normal for people to talk and chatter while going under anesthesia, but this was a bit much. I could hear the fear and it only created more fear in me. Then they went on the man next to me. Yet again, I had to listen to the entire procedure. I could hear the doctors attaching the electrodes to his head and checking the blood pressure cuff on his leg. I heard the doctor tell the nurses and those watching to back up, and he administered the shock. It took only seconds. They removed everything from his leg and head and pulled back my curtain. It was my turn. It felt a bit barbaric. It didn't seem like anyone viewed us as people, only patients that were there for a procedure.

I think they got so used to me being there and some of the formalities went off to the side. In the beginning, I was unaware of the electrodes and the blood pressure cuff because I was already under anesthesia when they applied these. When I came in and was second or third they were in a hurry and couldn't wait for me to be under anesthesia to apply the blood pressure cuff to my leg or the electrodes to my head. Not only did I have to listen to the other procedures happening, but I also had to view the other new staff watching my procedure like I was some zoo animal. They didn't address me or introduce themselves. I think they were new nurses learning the process. Why did they have to learn from me, I wondered. I felt like my personal space was so invaded and it was. There were two extra people watching along with the doctor and the regular nurse. I could hear the doctor explaining the steps of the procedure to the nurses. I could even feel, for the first time, the blood pressure cuff on my leg getting uncomfortably tight. Finally, the anesthesiologist showed up and administered my anesthesia. Up until I was out, I could hear the chatter and questions. I felt frightened and all alone. They didn't really pay any attention to me. It was all "a matter of fact". The human quality was gone. I kept asking myself if I really needed this.

The days I had the treatments I slept all day. I felt like I was just existing. I wasn't able to do much for myself. I had memory loss of the time around the treatments. I had minimal math skills (this was a side effect). Here is where time gets fuzzy or straight out not there. I know I had treatments over a 6- month period of time. I can remember having treatments during the summer, and when there was snow on the ground. My family could no longer take me to treatments, so I had to use a medical driver. So, during that time I went to have ECT by myself. Again, I would sleep the rest of the day if not the next day too. I still have short term memory difficulties today. I write myself notes in hopes to not forget important things.

After having shock treatments my family had to take care of me. They say it was like I had regressed as if I were a child needing taking care of. I wasn't able to cook for myself, or even stand on my two feet without bobbling around. They had to physically help me walk because I was so unstable on my feet. They thought I would stay like this. They feared I wouldn't regain the ability to live independently. They wondered if they would have to take care of me for the rest of my life. I can only imagine the fear in their hearts. No wonder they questioned a lot of my decisions. They were looking after me. I hope over the years they have found some peace in that I survived and can live a life with stability. I am sure there are times when they worry. I am grateful for their love and support; I know I am truly blessed.

Looking back, I am not sure if the ECT did anything beneficial. I think if I had more people around me maybe I could have ridden out the depression and not have gone to the extreme of shock treatments. I had become medication resistant. I had tried so many medications with little success. I guess there comes a time when I wondered if I would ever feel better or have normalcy in my life. I was told by a doctor that this was my last resort since I was not responding well to medications. I wish that I didn't have those treatments or have the need for them.

"15 Minute Appointment"

"You can't rush the river"

Unknown

After being hospitalized several times over many years I found a psychiatrist who would take me on as a patient. I didn't have any health insurance at the time. I paid cash when I could. This particular doctor was one I was working with while I was inpatient, Dr. Aron. He had a comfortable waiting room and office. He brought his dog, a Pomeranian named Shirley, into his sessions. He thought Shirley was calming for his client's. I thought it was cute and it didn't leave his side.

I would often show up early for my appointments. I happened to be in the process of moving out of NY and in with my dad for a short time, then to my sister's in Maryland, then with one guy, I was dating. What a disaster. He only wanted me to move in to help pay the heat bill. I had no real place to call home at the time.

I would sit in the waiting room filled with great sunlight, soft and comfortable chairs. There were a couple of doctors in the same suite sharing the same waiting room. As I awaited my appointment, I would watch others come and go. Some came and went more quickly than others. Some would come out with smiles and laughter and other in tears. I was somewhere in the middle.

I would often see the same girl in the waiting room. She was pretty, well dressed, hair done, wearing cute outfits and smiling. She would be called in before me. I once wondered if I had gotten my time wrong. How was she going in ahead of me? How long would I be waiting, especially since my appointment was always so long? 15 minutes later she comes out of the office all happy and smiles and laughter. I was called in next. I couldn't help but I ask with envy when would my appointments be only 15 minutes? My doctor looked at me and said that was going to take some time. He was not kidding. For many years to come and different doctors, my appointments were always quite lengthy. These appointments were for medication management, not talk therapy. We had to go over the medications I was on at that time. We discussed any side effects I was having. It feels like I was always experiencing some negative side effects to the medications. This was frustrating for me. I think I linked the length of my appointment with the stability of my illness.

Over about 5 years I saw several different doctors for medication management. Most of my appointments consisted of adding or changing medications. I became so over medicated. I was so sedated. I couldn't think for myself. I am not sure how I drove myself around. So much of that time is still quite a blur.

I moved from Maryland where I was living with my sister back to Connecticut with my new boyfriend and things began to fall into place. He was so kind and loving and patient with me. I then found a doctor in my area who took my insurance. I felt really comfortable with this doctor, Dr. Harold. He was an older gentleman and very well put together, listened really well and was very smart. He, thankfully, recognized that I was overmedicated. We put a plan in place to once again change my medication regimen. Over about a year I was taken off about 4-5 different drugs and only need to take 2-3 different ones. He even encouraged me to see a primary doctor and a gynecologist for routine appointments. The constant fog started to lift. I had more energy. I was beginning to sleep regular hours. I even lost 45 lbs. It took a few years, but I finally had appointments that lasted only 15 minutes. 15 minutes felt so great! I felt like had made a huge accomplishment with my medication. I only needed to do "check-in" appointments with Dr. Harold, finally, I had a true comprehension of the difference between a 55- minute appointment and a 15- minute appointment. I was so excited to reach a place where I was feeling more stable and able to manage my medications. My life was feeling more purposeful. It took a long time to get to have a 15- minute appointment. There are still times when I need a longer appointment depending on what is going on with me. I have a new appreciation for the 15- minute appointment and all that it means.

Looking back at the beginning of managing medications, I really had needed those longer appointments. It really took that long to check in on my life, medications, side effects, and overall health. Changes of medications became the norm, unfortunately. I experienced so many side effects that I didn't believe that I would ever be stable. I am thankful for Dr. Harold and all his patience with me. If I didn't have a good doctor, I am not sure where my life would be now or if I would even be alive.

Eating for Bipolar

"Our food should be our medicine and our medicine should be our food"
Hippocrates

Start where you are. When many of us look at nutrition and the food we put in our mouths it becomes another area for us to judge. We tell ourselves I am too fat, I am too skinny, my butt is too big, I need to lose weight, the judgements go on and on. Therefore, we all must start from where we are today, right now. What you ate or exercise you neglected no longer matters, it is in the past and that is not where you are going. We are only going forward.

It is so unfortunate that 80% of mentally ill are overweight. This can lead to other medical problems like cancer, cardiovascular disease, and diabetes.

In thinking about eating for bipolar, this statistic must take front and center. We need to be looking at eating for brain health, weight management, preventative nutrition. This is dealing with the physical side of your life. Since those of us with bipolar are all too often consumed with our mental health since it is always a factor.

Some may ask why are the mentally ill are overweight. Firstly, it is a side effect of many psychiatric medications. Side effects include sugar and carbohydrate cravings, physical and mental fatigue that can result in a sedentary lifestyle. So, with unhealthy food choices combined with the lack of activity and exercise the weight pours on.

I too have been affected by weight gain due to my medications. Before I was diagnosed, I weighed about 105 lbs. I wasn't trying to be this size; this is where my body sat naturally. I did exercise frequently though. On my first medication, I gained 10 lbs. in about two weeks. I went off that drug quickly. Over time and several medications changes, I put on weight without realizing since I was so focused on my mental health or lack of mental health. I came upon a photo of myself and wondered "who brought the fat girl?" It was a picture of me standing in front of my sister's Christmas tree about 50 lbs. overweight. It was like I saw myself for the first time.

Pictures don't lie. I had no recollection of that time. I don't remember being there at that time or how I got there since it was 7 hours away. I didn't even know who else had been there. So much was a blur, except for how much weight I had gained. I felt ashamed and embarrassed, and ugly. A few years later I went to Weight Watchers and lost 45 lbs. I was back at my normal healthy weight. I say healthy indicating that the higher weight was unhealthy because it was. My doctor was watching my blood pressure as it had become much higher for me. I prolonged taking blood pressure medication long enough to lose the weight and not need the medication. I was also having really bad constipation issues. I was always in pain with severe cramping. I had to see a gastrointestinal doctor to then have a colonoscopy. Thankfully, everything was normal and healthy. I didn't feel normal. The most puzzling part for me was that as my weight was increasing pound by pound no one said anything to me about it, that I remember. As my weight increased by 10's of pounds with each doctor appointment, why didn't they say something??? Weight is an issue that leads to so many other issues. I refuse to look at weight as something to be ashamed of. It is really a medical issue that needs to be addressed for what it is, extra weight. There are so many diets and meal plans. Some make claims to be a quick fix. Since weight is something I need to manage in a healthy way, I need to approach it in a way that's sustainable and manageable. A quick fix is just that, a quick fix. It is enticing but may be difficult to manage long-term.

Due to having to manage a mental illness, I try to look at food as medicine. When I sit and think about it, it makes sense. Think of times when you ate something, and you had a negative reaction. You could have experienced anything from a stomach ache, fatigue or even a full on an allergic reaction. Food is most often just something we put into our mouths when we are hungry without much thought.

Before we put something into our mouth, we should ask is this good for me? Does it have the potential to hurt or harm me? Many have experienced sugar highs and the crash in energy that it creates. This up and down of blood sugar can become dangerous in time. This is just one example.

Food cravings are something many people deal with. Some of us have a craving and we give into it without much thought. Food cravings happen for a reason, not because "I want chocolate". Cravings indicate that this is a time when you can look at what's going on with your body. A craving is usually because your body is lacking something. As you slowly feed your body the nutrients it requires, many cravings will go to the way-side.

There are many different thoughts on types of cravings and what they mean.

I have learned for myself and understand my cravings. I know when I have a craving for chocolate I need to add some extra magnesium by way of nuts, seeds, and vegetables. I have also used dark chocolate to put off my cravings. A little bit does the trick.

If I crave sugary foods I will drink a tall glass of water first. I will then have broccoli, grapes, cheese, chicken, fresh fruits, fatty fish, cabbage, cranberries, cauliflower, sweet potatoes, or spinach added to my next meal

If I have a craving for bread, pasta, and other carbs I will include high protein foods, red meat, fatty fish, nuts, beans, or chia seeds to my meals or as a snack that day.

I am lucky that I don't ever have cravings for salty or oily foods.

How do we eat healthily? That's often the big question, what do I eat? I know many people while seeking information on healthy foods to eat obtain a food list from their provider. This list is unmanageable for most, myself included. It doesn't work if you're told: "don't eat all these foods and do eat all these other foods". The average person doesn't know what kale is. Let's get realistic. To make lasting change the change must be slow and deliberate. I recommend adding a new food once a week. The week after that add another new food or a healthier option twice. Slowly you will crowd out the unhealthy foods by replacing them with healthier options.

Overall eating healthy is not that hard. I think we over complicate it. I recommend eating what makes you feel good and fills you without being stuffed. You may have to play with it until it suits your life. In each meal have a protein source and vegetable and some carbohydrate and healthy oils. The carbohydrate part is not an excuse to eat a donut or muffin. Carbohydrates are found in fruit, vegetables, and grains. These are healthier options for bread, rolls, and pastries.

Eating for the brain and boosting your brain power in easy and a must. Your brain requires nutrients just like your heart, lungs and muscles do. What foods are particularly good?

The following foods are known for brain health. These are foods that should be a staple in your eating and your life. Some of these foods may be new to some people and that is ok. You can start where you are and slowly add in these food items into your daily meal plans.

I understand that many people have food allergies. Some of the foods on this list might not be good for everyone. What is good for one person may not be good for another person. Be careful when adding new foods. Go slow and listen to your body.

Top 15 Brain Foods/Nutrients:

1. Avocados – This fruit is one of the healthiest ones you can eat. This is full of the healthy fats and keeps blood sugar levels steady. They help prevent blood clots in the brain and improve cognitive function including memory and concentration. They help to protect against stroke. They have the highest protein and lowest sugar content of any fruit.

2. Eat oily fish – Main sources of oily fish are salmon, trout, mackerel, herring, and sardines to name the most common. Your brain needs Essential Fatty Acids which cannot be produced by the body, therefore, must come from your diet and supplementation. The most effective omega-3's occurred naturally in oily fish in the form of EPA and DHA. There are plant sources also such as flaxseed, pumpkin seeds, walnuts and their oils. These fats, are important for brain health and function. Receiving sufficient amounts of these fats can help manage stress and aids in the production of serotonin, a good mood brain chemical.

3. Blueberries – are studied and suggest that they improve and reduce short term memory loss. The darker the better. They contain anthocyanins which fight free radicals and can offer anti-inflammatories, anti-viral, and anti-cancer benefits.

4. Tomatoes – They contain lycopene, which is a powerful anti-oxidant, and fights free-radicals, and help prevent cancer.

5. Vitamin B-rich foods – chicken, eggs and leafy greens are high in vitamin B. These vitamins help you to have lasting energy, and great for nerve health.

6. Broccoli - is a great source of vitamin K which is known to enhance cognitive function and improve brain-power. Broccoli definitely gives you the biggest bang for your buck in regards to nutrients.

7. Pumpkin Seeds – They are high in zinc which is vital for enhancing memory and thinking skills. They are also high in magnesium which helps reduce stress and tryptophan.

8. Beets – This root vegetable is the most nutritious plant that you can eat. They are full of antioxidants that clean the blood of toxins and are protective against cancer. They increase blood flow to the brain aiding in performance.

9. Bone Broth – This is the ultimate food for healing the gut and in turn healing the brain. It reduces and prevents intestinal inflammation, helps keep the immune system working properly and helping to improve memory.

10. Celery - Has high levels of antioxidants and have natural anti-inflammatories to aid in joint pain, and IBS. It is extremely nutrient dense, loaded with vitamins and minerals.

11. Coconut Oil – It is one of the most versatile foods. It is a natural anti-inflammatory, suppressing inflammatory cells. It can help with memory loss with aging and kills the bad bacteria in the gut.

12. Dark Chocolate – at least 70% of cocoa can be good for you. It has anti-inflammatory properties and can help to lower blood pressure and improve blood flow to the brain.

13. Extra Virgin Olive Oil – This has properties that improve learning and memory. It can also reverse the age and disease related changes.

14. Turmeric – this is an ancient root that has been used through history for its healing properties. It contains the most powerful anti-inflammatories. It improves the brain's oxygen intake, keeping you alert and able to process information.

15. Walnuts – Eating just a few a day can improve your cognitive health. They have very high levels of antioxidants, vitamins, and minerals. They can also improve mental alertness.

Mindbodygreen website summarizes that new research has linked gut health and mental health. There is data that supports the existence of the gut-brain axis. This is the communication area between your brain and your gut. This is thought to be a two-way connection that can experience a disruption and affects the gut and brain health.

It is important to maintain gut health since it also affects most of your body systems. A healthy gut can affect the metabolism of fats and proteins along with certain vitamins. I personally take probiotic supplements on a daily basis.

I hate to be the one to tell you, but Sugar is NOT your friend.

"Like heroin, cocaine, and caffeine, sugar is an addictive, destructive drug, yet we consume it daily in everything from cigarettes to bread." William Dufty, author of "Sugar Blues".

The average American consumes more than 100 pounds of sugar and sweeteners yearly. As humans, we love sweet things. It is a simple carbohydrate that occurs naturally in food like grains, beans, vegetables, and fruit.

Joshua Rosenthal, "Integrative Nutrition", 2008 writes that refined table sugar, also called sucrose, is very different. Sucrose is extracted from either sugarcane or beets. Sucrose lacks vitamins, minerals, and fiber thus requiring extra effort for the body to digest. The body must deplete its own store of minerals and enzymes to absorb sucrose properly. Instead of providing the body with the nutrition it creates a deficiency. It enters the bloodstream quickly and wreaks havoc on the blood sugar levels. It pushes the levels sky-high causing increased energy, excitability, nervous tension and even hyperactivity. After the sugar high, blood sugar levels plummet extremely low causing fatigue, depression, exhaustion, and overall yucky feeling.

People may realize that their body reacts to sugar, but they fail to realize that it also creates an emotional roller coaster. People who have mood disorders should evaluate their nutritional intake to prevent highs and lows from our foods, something we can control. According to Rosenthal sugar actually qualifies as an addictive substance for the following reasons 1. Eating even small amounts creates a desire for more. 2. Suddenly quitting eating sugar causes withdrawal symptoms like headaches, mood swings, cravings, and fatigue.

Sugar is not just sugar anymore. There are many names and forms of sugars that the average person in unaware of. Food companies have found inventive ways to incorporate sugar into their foods to enhance flavor and make you come back for more!

The following is a list of the many names of sugar: brown sugar, confectioner's sugar or powdered sugar, corn syrup, dextrose or glucose, high-fructose corn syrup, honey, invert sugar (which is a mixture of glucose and fructose), lactose or milk sugar, levulose or fructose, raw sugar, sorbitol, mannitol, malitol, xylitol, sucrose or table sugar, and turbinado sugar.

Not only is sugar an issue for most people, but artificial sweeteners are even worse. The FDA has approved many artificial sweeteners, leading the public in thinking they are a safe alternative to sugar, in which they are not. There are five categories of artificial sweeteners that are FDA approved: 1. Aspartame, sold under the brand names NutraSweet and Equal 2: Saccharin, sold under the brand name Sweet'n low 3. Sucralose, sold under the brand name Splenda 4. Acesulfame K, made from a german chemical company, used in foods, beverages and pharmaceutical products. 5. Neotame, produced by Nutrasweet Company used in diet soft drinks and, low calorie foods.

There are many negative medical symptoms that occur from the intake of artificial sweeteners. Fortunately, most symptoms can be alleviated when discontinued. Some of the symptoms include headaches, blurred vision, memory loss, nausea, the ringing of the ears, hyperactivity, G.I. issues, PMS, increased appetite, skin lesions, fatigue, insomnia, mood changes, depression, joint pain, numbness and tingling of extremities to name a few.

Since there is such a high rate of obesity among the mentally ill due to medications, here are some popular weight loss tips:

1. Drink water. Hunger is often confused with dehydration. Drink a glass of water before you reach for a snack. Also, drinking a glass of water prior to each meal can help you to eat less. Be sure to drink plenty of water a day, and reduce soda, caffeine, and alcoholic beverages.

2. Eat "real" carbohydrates. Replace white bread, pastries, cereals with fruits and vegetables, along with whole grains, seeds, nuts, and legumes. These can help stabilize sugar levels in the bloodstream and decreases mood swings.

3. Eat Healthy Fats. Fats are not to be feared and they do not cause you to gain fat. Our body uses dietary fat for energy, hair and skin health, vitamin absorption, and bodily functions. Healthy fats that come from nuts, seeds, fish, avocados, and extra virgin olive oil protect us from heart disease, cancer, and depression and they can naturally lower cholesterol.

4. Eat lean proteins. Proteins are essential for cellular growth and renewal. It aids in blood sugar stabilization and energy. Foods that contain protein are meat, dairy, eggs, fish and plant sources like nuts and seeds.

5. Always Eat Breakfast. By eating breakfast, you jumpstart your metabolism and helps reduce cravings. Studies show that eating breakfast helps to maintain a healthy body weight.

6. Eat Frequently. Eat throughout the day. This will help maintain blood sugar levels and prevent cravings and binge eating. By eating often your body knows there is food

coming in and will be more able to let go of fat as it won't feel starved.

7. Exercise. This helps lead to decreased body weight, healthy blood pressure, and improved mood. Take the opportunity to walk and move your body as often as you can, for example, take the stairs and not the elevator.

8. Sleep. The lack of sleep can disrupt your body's rhythms leading to fatigue, lower metabolism, and an overactive appetite. It is recommended to sleep 7-8 hours nightly. If sleep is an issue try drinking chamomile tea in the evening, reading before bed but no electronics. Artificial light can disrupt your sleeping patters. In the evening try turning off televisions, computers, cell phones to prevent too many stimuli in the evening hours.

9. Cook your own food. When you cook your own meals, you know what is in your food and what exactly you are eating. Eating at home allows for more portion control thus preventing overeating. Instead of the hidden salts and sugars, cooking your own meals allows you to cut unnecessary calories.

10. Keep track of what you eat. By tracking what you eat you reduce the chance of artificial ingredients that can lead to medical problems. Be sure to read all of your food labels. If you can't pronounce an ingredient in your food, or there is a laundry list of ingredients don't eat them. There is always a more natural source of food to eat.

My Always

"To the love of my life, even though we will die take comfort in knowing that our love never will"

gemma troy

Following my diagnosis and the years to come were the most difficult time in my life. Maybe it is good that I have some memory loss around that time. Through all the instabililty I experienced with my illness, I met an incredible man. He didn't judge me or ask questions. He brought me candy when I was in the hospital. He told me very early after we met that he would always be my friend and be there for me. He has yet to go back on those words he said 13 years ago. I truly believe there was divine work at play here. When he and I first met, he told me stories about where he was from. Ironically, my sister happened to be living down the street from where he grew up in a family of 7 children, in another state in a different part of the country. I knew of the places he spoke of. I knew of the local bar that everyone went to. We talked about the bridge that connected Solomons Maryland to the other side. He had played on it as a kid while it was being built. He was funny and caring. He has beautiful blue eyes, and young skin with a devious smile. He was kind and yet rough around the edges. He is a no bull shit kind of man. He would watch silly TV shows with me, even though they weren't his cup of tea. We would play cards and I think he let me win sometimes. There were times that I was barely hanging on and had a lot of difficulties doing the regular day to day activities. One morning he called me early and told me to open my door. I opened my door to find a couple bags of groceries. There was milk, fruit and even toilet paper. I couldn't believe he did that for me, and in the early hours before he went to work. That is the kindest thing anyone has ever done for me.

We had a lot of bumps in the road early on, due to my instability. I am grateful we got through the hell we once experienced. I feel blessed by his selflessness. He never gave up on me!! I truly believe he saved my life. He openly gave me his home and in time his heart. Together we built a really safe place for me to live and heal. He guarded me against any additional stressors. He really protected me and my mind. It was many years until I started to experience any kind of stability. I was lucky, he gave me unconditional support with no expectations. He didn't ask or expect me to do anything, not cook or clean or anything. I mostly slept as I juggled with finding the right combination of medication. He prepared all my meals. He did my laundry and took me to my appointments. He gave me a gift no one else could- he gave me a way back to myself. I feel like I am one of the lucky ones. Not everyone gets a quiet safe place to heal and recover without having to focus on anything else. I moved into his apartment and we grew in love in a place in which we both now call home.

I have learned to love unconditionally and to accept love. He is mine forever and always.

Stability

"You never know what weapons you've got until you go through pain more than flesh and blood can stand"

Suri Singh

Stability is defined as the state or quality of being stable, firmness in position, and/or without change.

I like the continuance without change. Ideally, this is what we strive for. Unfortunately, it takes a lot of work to be stable. Medication is usually the first line of defense. It may take several different medications to find the one, or ones that help the most. Very importantly, work with your doctor to find a combination of medications that work well for you. I had the misfortune of changing several drugs at once. I didn't know which drug was helping me and which one was not. For me, it took anywhere from 4-6 weeks to know if a drug was going to help alleviate my symptoms. Sometimes I notice a difference in a few days. However, if I change more than one drug at a time I have no idea what is working and what is not. Each drug comes with its own side effects. Some I had and some I didn't. Most commonly I experienced dry mouth or weight gain.

From my original diagnosis of bipolar I with rapid cycling and PTSD, it took me about 5 years to reach any type of stability. The first five years of my diagnosis were absolutely horrid!! The illness became debilitating. I lost my life as I had known it. I lost my life in NY when my dad moved me back to Connecticut to live with him. I lost all my friends, I lost my sense of humor, I had no idea if or when it would get any better. I don't pretend that this is an easy journey. It's just that, a journey, a process. You need to have patience with yourself. Don't beat yourself up when things don't work the first time, or second, or third. Be kind to yourself because this is probably the most difficult thing you will endure in your lifetime.

When I talk about stability, it may look a bit different for everyone. For me, stability meant I could pay my bills without bouncing checks all over town. I was also able to cook meals, do laundry (which I am still not very good with), and grocery shopping. I know it sounds like the basics, and it is. As more time passed and I stayed on the same medication, I was able to participate in my own life again. I regained interest in things I had previously enjoyed, I was able to connect with the creative side of myself through baking and quilting. It feels really good to be able to finish a project or read a book from beginning to end.

There are definitely "relapses" along the way. I think many people experience them. I know what they feel like, how different I feel and how my thoughts and behaviors change. Some come on quickly, others can take days or even weeks to manifest. There are times when those around me have made me aware of behavioral changes. I admit that these times suck! I then wonder if I have made a fool of myself and not realized it.

It's kind of unbelievable that my behavior and actions can change, and I am one of the last to know. There are times when I feel things just aren't right and have to go from there. I start where I am at, at that particular time. I really pay attention to my spending habits. These tell-tale signs that things are about to or are going array. I try to keep receipts, so I know where what, and how much I have spent. This is helpful, but not fool proof.

I feel so frustrated at times. I feel like things were going well and then bang...... things are not going well. I am lucky to have support around me. I am able to pick up on my mood changes before too much damage is done. My first relapse, after many years of stability, was triggered by having surgery myself and then traveling across the country to help my sister with her surgery. I then got physically sick with bronchitis. All this at the same time caused me to relapse. I was agitated, I opened new credit cards, after having only using cash, this felt like a free treat. I spent over $8000.00 in credit cards within a few months. I couldn't focus, I wasn't participating in my daily activities, I was not doing any daily cleaning. I let things build up. I wasn't taking my medication the same. I was cracking pills in half, taking extra doses trying to feel better. When I finally went to the doctor, I was only a few days away from needing to be hospitalized. I think I saw my doctor's head spin when I told him everything that had been going on and what I was doing with my medication. After figuring everything out and adjusting my medication, I was on my way back to having stability. It did take several months. Like I said, this is a process.

one bipolar person to another:

Yes, medications may be needed to regain stability in your life. They are not the only thing. Talk therapy is very helpful and I strongly recommended it. Therapy can help you to find any underlying issues that may have triggered your illness and/or relapses. Therapists can be a good line of defense. When you are feeling better, you can forget how to nip things in the bud. They will pick up on things that you may overlook or just haven't noticed yet. I cannot imagine not having my therapist. To this day I have a standing weekly appointment with my therapist. Regardless of how stable I may feel, I keep this standing appointment.

I have found that self-care is very important to my mental health. It is different for everyone, and some don't do any kind of self-care. Whatever type of care that you do for yourself may help you to feel better. Getting a massage, facials, acupuncture or other therapies are very beneficial. Some people carve out time in the daily or weekly schedule for meditation, yoga, or even journaling. It can be just about anything. I feel that any type of self-care one can do for themselves is most important. On a regular basis we put out our energy whether it's a job, care taking and teaching- we need to refuel, or we could break down. Have you ever noticed that people who are often stressed come down with the most colds or a virus? As a whole, we need to have some type of self-care to keep us going, keep us healthy and keep us available to others.

Exercise can really compliment other therapies. The good thing about exercise is that it is free!!! You can walk or run outside. You can also find groups to exercise with, a boot camp class or join a club (not free but may have more of what you need). When the weather doesn't cooperate, you can find a local mall and walk around. Exercise has been recommended by my doctors and has proven to be very beneficial to my mental state. Exercise releases endorphins in the brain. These are happy things. Also, the feeling of accomplishing something physical is very rewarding. Exercise can also help with some of the unwanted side effects of medications. I find I feel much better when I exercise.

The great thing about exercise is that you can start at any time in your life. My mother is now 70 years old. She has not exercised for over 15 years. She has recently begun walking. She is already feeling the positive effects of the exercise. It has become a daily habit that she feels must get done. She is able to do far more than she thought she was capable of. When we push ourselves, it is amazing what we can accomplish. I have to admit, I am very proud of her.

While trying to find some sort of stability, you really need to focus on other facets of your life, not just your illness. This illness takes so much from you and is so difficult at times that it can be easy to forget there are other areas of our lives. Some people find solace in religion or spirituality. Meditation is helpful in calming the mind and can help refocus our thoughts. There are so many different types of meditation. There are guided vocal meditations, instrumental, and sometimes you can focus on counting your breaths. A few minutes at a time goes a long way.

Another thing you could look at is your home environment. Are things in order or are they a mess? Is it calming or overwhelming? Is your bed made? Are the dishes done? Do you know where your keys are? Is your fridge full or empty? Do you have enough milk for your coffee? These may sound like simple nuances, but they are important. You cannot feel healthy if your surroundings are a mess. If this all seems too overwhelming, pick one thing at a time. Try to make your bed daily. It's one activity that doesn't take a lot of time, but it's a step toward things looking nice and in order. Write yourself a note of one thing you want to accomplish daily. This will help you feel like you are able to complete something. That goes along way with your self-esteem.

Another thing to look at is your finances. This can cause so much unwanted anxiety. I know many people are on disability and funds are low. While on disability, there are many benefits you can receive. You can contact your local Social Services and may qualify for energy assistance, food assistance, even housing. If you have medical assistance, make sure you are utilizing all the benefits you are allowed, such as eye care and dental. If your finances are a wreck like mine have been, set up small things to take care of. One of the most important things you can do for your credit it to pay your bills on time. If this is not possible, call the company to make payment arrangements for yourself. You don't have to hide from your bill collectors. I would answer the phone and pretend I was someone else, so the collectors didn't know it was me. I even had my sister call some of my bill collectors pretending to be me and set up payment arrangements for me. She was so good at it. Many will try to work with you in some way. Set financial priorities. You obviously need a roof over your head, electricity, heat, a phone. The basics. You need to have these organized and up to date. This is another way you can get your control back and feel like you can accomplish something important. I keep all my monthly bills in a notebook. I make a list of my regular monthly bills with the amounts and due dates. This usually works like a charm. Using my notebooks and online banking helps me so much. I don't think I ever learned to balance a check book.

How are your relationships with your family? How are your relationships with friends, parents, siblings, your extended family? We all deal with the relationships inside of our home, but how are the ones outside of your home? Have you neglected them? Having and keeping relationships while dealing with a mood disorder is very hard. This outside world can play a very important role in your daily life. Many people who suffer from a mood disorder have alienated themselves from those around them. Behaviors or reactions to outside situations may not have been ideal. You may feel like you embarrassed yourself or significant others which results in isolation. It is easy to fall into this trap of isolation. Those close to you know what's going on for the most part in some way or another. Remember, they were your friend before you got sick. Your siblings still love you even though the relationship may be strained due to your illness. If you let go, the embarrassment or the things that hold you back you may be able to keep and/or regain those relationships. You have an illness. Yes, I know it is not like the average illness since it involves your mood and behaviors from those moods, but it is still an illness you must maneuver for the rest of your life. On days when you don't feel so bad try to reach out to those strained relationships to re-build them. You may want to explain how you have been feeling and how you have been managing. If you let them know you appreciate them and their relationship and their support, you might be surprised. Most people are consumed with their own lives. They may not know the depths in which you struggle or any progress you may have made. Allow them in. Allow them to see you vulnerable. You are still a person too with the similar thoughts and feelings and dreams that others have. It is very uplifting when you stop hiding and worry about being judged. Life is a long time. We are social beings therefore, we don't do life well alone. You don't deserve to be punished or looked down upon because you have an illness. Society doesn't sit in judgement of a cancer patient. We cannot allow them to sit in judgement of a mental illness. Empower yourself and try to revive those hurt or neglected relationships.

One thing I found out about myself is that I have a creative side. I taught myself to quilt. It felt so productive to finish a quilt. I made about a dozen of them in a year's time. I just completed my own bedroom curtains. It's relaxing and helps me focus on a task. I also love to bake and decorate cakes. This came to me so naturally. I took a decorating class and I was off and running. I did a really large cake for a non-profit that benefits ill children. That felt really good! There are times when I don't bake at all. I find when I do bake it relaxes me. I can put all my focus into something other than myself. It's very rewarding, especially when it tastes good.

Because there happens to me a mental diagnosis, we often forget about physical health. Make sure you're not forgetting yearly physicals along with routine blood work. Some medications can alter bodily functions. Some will increase sugar levels, others may cause your body temperature difficult to regulate in the heat. For women, do not neglect the "girl parts" and routine mammograms. These are very helpful for early detection of medical issues. Dealing with a mental illness is plenty enough, we don't need physical ailments sneaking up on us. We don't need the added stress.

Ask around and try to find a physician that listens to you and is on your side. Since most of us with bipolar disorder will have to be on medications for a lifetime, physical health becomes even more important. There happens to be a lengthy list of side effects from psychiatric medications. You need to have a supportive and caring primary physician. The more you can do for your physical health, the better your mental health can be.

Love Yourself

Nobody tells you

It is okay to call yourself beautiful

It is okay to smile in mirrors

And it is perfectly fine

To say your own eyes are pretty

It is wonderful to love your waist

And your legs

Regardless of their size

And you are not conceited

If you use your fingers to list

Everything you're good at

Rather than point at all your own flaws

You can acknowledge you're smart

And that you will go places

And you will be someone

Greater than your mistakes

You can't always expect other people to believe in yourself for you

(AKR)

Be Kind to Yourself

Rid yourself of negative self-talk. If you are consumed with negative self-thoughts, you need to replace those with positive self- talk. What you think you will manifest.

You need to believe in yourself. There may be a time where you have to "fake it till you make it". Continuous negative thoughts will only bring you down and make it more difficult to have positivity and stability.

I am sure through your illness you have heard others tell you that "you can't". I have! You may have been told your damaged. You may have been told to make other plans for your life, not what you've dreamed of. You may have been told that you shouldn't have children. You may have been told that society won't trust you, they won't believe in you. All the "cant's" are completely untrue!!

I am in no way making excuses for others. However, when family and friends speak "off the cuff", they really have no idea where those words will land. They do not understand the impact of their words. Sometimes we may have to educate them for our own good.

Having an illness of any kind is hard enough. Having an illness that you cannot see and is full of stigmas and judgments makes it all that much harder. Unfortunately, you will have to learn to set up healthy boundaries. I don't think others are purposely trying to hurt you, they just don't understand. By setting boundaries for yourself and those around you will help yourself to stay strong, and able to say "no".

You must regularly remind yourself that you are worthy of anything you may dream of. You have the power to make your own reality. If you continually tell yourself that you are not good enough, strong enough, smart enough, or pretty enough then you never will. That is why negative self-talk is so detrimental to your health. Negative self- talk creates a reality in which you are destined to fail because that is what you tell yourself is the best you can be.

Talk to yourself with kind and loving words, ONLY!! Tell yourself YES!! Yes, you are deserving. Yes, you will feel better. Yes, you can be productive. Your life depends on it. Take quotes or pictures that make you smile or laugh and put them all around you. Make sure you can see them regularly.

Have self- compassion! Unfortunately, it is often overlooked. We have compassion for others. We want to be there for loved ones. In being there for others you forget to be there for yourself. While trying to find or maintain some type of stability, you must know it is ok to focus on yourself. You must.

Self- compassion is extending compassion to yourself in times of feeling inadequacy, failure, or overall suffering.

This is not a pity party or having self-pity. This is offering you understanding and kindness when things do not go the way you intended.

Having bipolar disorder at any stage, your mind often heads toward negativity and self-deprivation. When you find yourself in this tornado of negative feelings, you must fight your hardest fight, to find something positive to hold onto. This is definitely an inner battle within you. Your illness is creating a world wind of emotions and thoughts within you. This is not the time to go to bed. This is the time to remind yourself that you will not always feel this bad. You have to look for a glimmer of light that you can grasp on to, if only for a few minutes. I say a few minutes because it really is minute to minute at times. You need to break down your negativity and emptiness into little blocks of time. As a minute passes, then 15 minutes, then a half an hour, and an hour, you can see how you have fought through this time and know it to be a success. Baby steps and faking it until you make it. Be kind to yourself while trying to find stability.

Please Love Yourself so someone else can.

This is an exercise to get to know yourself. Ways to Love Yourself and be loved.

How many times do you look in the mirror and not like what you see? What do you feel? Do you even know who that person is that you don't like?

So many of us go through life not loving the person we are, but do we know why??

It is time to DIG!!!! What I am going to ask you to do next may not be easy but much needed.

It is time to look back on your life, kind of like a picture book, and really see what has hurt you. Really hurt you. Were you bullied as a child? Did someone tell you that you can't? Did someone take your power away from you? Did someone physically or sexually hurt you? Were you lied to, taken advantage of?

We walk around our daily lives in pain. Whether the pain is emotional or physical, we don't always know. Sometimes things get jumbeled around in your head and you don't know what it is you feel. Maybe you are numb or fight back the tears. Either way, it is time to love yourself. Some of you may have never loved yourself or known how.

Back to the person in the mirror. Look at that person. Don't judge, just look. What do you see? Start with the top of your head and work down. Don't worry about the size of the mirror because it doesn't matter. What are you seeing? Acknowledge this person, say hello. It will feel silly at first, and that is ok. No one else is watching, just you and the mirror.

Look at the color of your hair. Do you like it? Do you want to change it? If you want to change it do you know why? Is it too light or too dark? Or maybe its showing your age and stress with grays. How do you feel when you look at your hair? Be honest, this is not the time to lie to yourself. What do you think your hair says about you? Not what you think others may think, only you. Some people hide behind their hair. The color is really dramatic, the length too long, not styled or taken care of. This can be used to keep people at bay. Some think they are safe if they don't have to interact with others, therefore purposefully let themselves go. Do Not Hold your Tears Back!!! Hair is kind of funny. If its styled and a color you like it can really lift your spirits. If you want to change the color, length or style go for it! When you decide to make a change make sure you do it for yourself and only yourself.

Look into your eyes. Look at the color and the shape. Are your eyes bright or do they look tired and tell a story? The eyes are the window to your soul. They hold so much expression and often are a tell for what you are thinking. Don't look away, really look into your eyes. What is the story your eyes are telling you? Are tears falling? Don't hold them back, let them flow. Some people think that if they let themselves cry they won't stop. You will stop, I promise. So again, what is going on in those eyes? What have they seen? What have they closed up tight to not see? Look into your eyes and tell yourself that it is all ok. Look into your eyes and forgive yourself. Look into your windows of your soul and love what you see. Love the look in your eyes. Whether you are laughing or crying, love the eyes you see. Acknowledge the beautiful color that they are. Your eye color is unique to you. It makes you special. Allow your eyes to open up and take in the light. Trust that your eyes are a beautiful expression of who you are.

This may sound silly but look at your nose. Is it short or long, straight or crooked? Does your nose tell a story? Is it crooked because it was injured, or was it born that way? If it was hurt, how? Do you remember? Did you get hit by something or someone? You might originally have thought this was a silly thing to focus on, your nose. Your nose does so much for you, not just the physical look of it. It allows you to smell beautiful flowers in the spring, a new rainfall, snowfall, freshly cut grass. It also smells fowl things like rotten foods, poops left in the yard by the dog. Your nose also protects you. Your nose smells smoke that warns you of a fire. It also tries to protect you from daily allergens like pollen or perfume. Again, was it injured? Really look at the shape of it. Do you even like it? Do you have difficulty breathing through it? Does your nose remind you of something or someone? Does it make you cry? It is ok if your brought to tears, let them flow. If you are full of tears, what is causing them, a memory? Don't hold back whatever emotions come up. This is the time to let them go. No one is watching you, it is only you. There is no judging. You need to let these emotions out. You may need to cry. Sometimes a cry involves your whole body. That is great! You need to let all these emotions flow and cry like never before.

Look at your smile. Wait, so do you even smile? Do you have a natural pout? Do you love smiling? When you smile you welcome those around you, "Smile and the whole world smiles with you..." It is so true. A smile is contagious, and you can give it to others, literally. When someone walks by and you look at them and smile, they usually smile back. You not only feel good from smiling, you gave someone else a good feeling by simply smiling.

 It can be difficult to smile sometimes. There are times when you fake a smile. Do you think others realize your faking? A faked smile could come off as sarcastic. This is definitely not what you want to portray. Back to the mirror. Are you trying to smile? Does it hurt to smile, you know what I mean. Your face can "hurt" from trying to smile. Your face can hurt from smiling a lot. Which "hurt" do you choose? Does trying to smile make you sad, bring you to tears? This may be the first time you realized that you don't smile much. Do you feel sad inside when you look at your smile and it doesn't look or feel real? Its ok. You can notice it now and begin to make changes. First, you need to acknowledge the feelings that arise while looking at the smile on your face. Feel these feelings. Don't push them aside. This is very important. Your smile talks to the world, whether you have realized before now or not. Go along with any and all emotions that come up. This is really time to embrace those feelings. Get to know them. Make friends with all the different emotions you feel. By recognizing and becoming comfortable with your feelings you can then start to heal the hurts you feel.

Misconceptions

"The process informs the destination"

Unknown

There are several misconceptions about bipolar disorder. The misconceptions can make it difficult for someone to seek help. Firstly, you may need medication. There are a lot of false information stating that you, having bipolar disorder, do not need medication. There are books, websites, blogs all telling whoever their readers are that they can heal this disorder with vitamins or nutrition or different "healing" modalities. I have read many of these. I have also consulted with several doctors and therapist, all confirming that those with bipolar disorder do indeed need medication. No one wants to be on medication, me being one of them. If someone is determined in finding information against medication, you can find what you seek. Unfortunately, most bipolar patients require medication. We can deny and fight it all we want, medication is still needed. The sooner you accept this reality, the closer you are to feeling better.

All psychiatrists are not the same and don't provide the same level of care. This is very unfortunate. When we seek a psychiatrist during a crisis we trust what they have to say. We often take what they prescribe. I think everyone had a different introduction to psychiatric medication. They are not usually the happiest of times. So, we are given medication from that provider, but they don't usually become your regular doctor. Many of us have had to take whatever is available, whoever takes the insurance you have. Some will work on a "sliding scale", meaning they will work with their patient on cash payments.

How to find a good one comes by recommendation or pure luck. There really should be a better set up. However, when trying to find a psychiatrist make sure you make a list of questions to ask. If you don't make a list, you can be in and out and on your way to the car and your question pops up. Too late, you have to wait till next appointment. You need to know how available they are. Do they have an answering service when they are not in the office? How do they handle the crisis, what is their protocol, how quickly can you anticipate them to return your phone calls? You might wonder why I have focused you here. This information is very important. Indeed, you should ask questions about medication. Your care does not and should not stop when you walk out the door. You need to be able to have a proper care in a crisis, or between appointments.

I have had some bad psychiatrists. I say they are bad because of the way in which they handled things, if at all. I had one doctor that liked to change my medications 2 and 3 at a time. No wonder why I ended up in the hospital during just about every medication change. For me, I now know medications should only be changed one at a time.

After being released from an inpatient hospital I continued with the ECT on an outpatient basis. During this time, they required I attend an outpatient program. It made no sense to me then and still doesn't. So, they had it set up that I saw an appointed psychiatrist, therapist, and group therapy. There was no consistency. I saw over 4 different psychiatrists during this program, and they all had a different regime. I had to take what was given. From there I bounced around from psychiatrist to psychiatrist. Finally, about 6 years after that chaos I found a wonderful doctor. He was kind, upfront about his policies, very smart and knowledgeable about my illness. He even encouraged and suggested that I see a primary doctor and a gynecologist. All great suggestions. He was treating more than my illness, he was treating me as a whole person. At the time, I didn't realize how important it was to have a doctor that would encourage me to treat my whole person.

Another misconception is thinking that all people with bipolar disorder are violent. Not all people with this illness are violent. In cases where violence occurs, there is usually brought on by something, whether it be environmental or organic. When a medication change occurs, the individual can have a bad reaction it can bring on anger, agitation, or sometimes violence. Alcohol is also a contributing factor for violence. Medication and alcohol do not mix well. Severe trauma or a major unseen life change can bring on violence. Yes, it can occur, just not for everyone.

It is thought that if a person has bipolar disorder, they cannot hold down a job. Again, this is untrue. If a person is stable they can be productive, and even quite successful. Most people who suffer from this illness aren't broadcasting it at work in fear of discrimination. So, it is difficult for the average person to recognize that someone has bipolar disorder unless they tell you, or you are witness to some type of crisis. Unfortunately, many people suffer from relapses. During this time, it can be next to impossible to keep up with a "job". You may want to put things in place in case of a relapse. Planning for the future is important and difficult all at the same time. If someone has a job pre-planning is important. If you have children, you need something or someone in place to help and assist until you regain your stability. Some people with careers may have an open dialogue with their superior or boss. If your job provides benefits you can accumulate you're sick and/or vacation time for when a relapse occurs. Fortunately, there are several protections for people with mental illnesses including the Americans with Disabilities Act (ADA) and the equal Employment Opportunity Act. Both acts prohibit discrimination against people with disabilities in the workplace. When you're in a tough time it's almost impossible to see down the line to plan for the future. So, when you're feeling well is the time to plan for the worst. You may never need it, but it's there none the less.

Personally, I have found it next to impossible to hold down a regular job. For me in the past is has been the culprit for instability in my moods, thus leaving be open to relapse. I have tried several different jobs in the past with no success. So, now I know it is not a healthy thing for me to try and do. There are times when I think things are going well and I feel stable and I convince myself into thinking I can get a job. Then, I sit and think of all the things that will accompany a job, and all the responsibilities that come along with a job. I realize that I am unable to meet those demands on a regular basis. For me, I know it is not something I can do, but others may be quite capable.

Another misconception is that you cannot control bipolar disorder. In a way, this is a half- truth and depends on how you define "control". Bipolar disorder can be managed, and stability can be reached. If you have stability, you have some control over your moods, but it's really about management. It really isn't about control, it's about reaching stability and managing that on a daily basis.

Conclusion

"In the ashes of my old dreams arose a light that lit the path towards my soul's mission »

Souldipity

I have really come through the storm. I am a healthier, happier, and stronger woman than before. I have a good relationship with myself, even on the trying days. When I have an off day, I know it won't last forever, it is only temporary, and I must remind myself of that. I am surviving!! Every day brings a new and unexpected challenge. I now have the tools and support to deal with daily disruptions.

Having support during an illness is so important and such a gift. Being supportive of someone with a mental illness is quite difficult. I imagine it is very hard to watch your loved one struggle with their mind. Loving someone with bipolar is like watching a roller coaster go by and by with no end in sight. I felt the same way, except I was the one on the roller coaster. My moods kept going around and around up and down. My moods were literally going up to a state of euphoria and then down to a deep desperate depression.

This illness takes everyone down a different path. Sure, the symptoms are similar, but no two experiences it in the same way. What is the same, we all have family that is affected in one way or another? I know my family went through hell and back with me. They had to sacrifice time, money, sweat and tears. I am grateful they tried as hard as they could. I honestly don't remember some of the worst times, maybe that's a blessing in disguise. I know my family remembers. They fought for me. My Dad came to see me in more hospitals than he probably wants to count.

My family did what they could without much guidance. I remember my sister saved my life more than once. I can only imagine the fear she felt when she fought the fight that I couldn't. Without her, I would not be here today. I truly, from the depths of my heart, cherish her, and our relationship. I am grateful for the love she has for me and me for her.

Not everyone has the support that I did through the toughest of times. I do know how lucky I am. Those who suffer from a mental illness often suffer alone, not aware of the support available to them. I am not one to tell others what to do. I will openly share my story. It is just that, my story. Everyone struggles differently. No two are the same. What is the same, is the pain and despair that is felt when you are not sure which way to turn, or where to go for help. We have to hold on the belief that as bad as things are now, or how bad we feel today it won't last forever. There will be better days. You have to hold on to the hope and believe there is light at the end of the tunnel.

My whole life I knew I wanted to write a book. I would struggle with the topic, what I would write about. As I found myself writing this book I realized that I hadn't lived enough life with enough experience to write it before now. I needed to go through all I went through to have any impact on someone else's life and struggles. Looking back, I probably would have rather an easier path, one with less depravity and struggle, none the less. This was my path to bear. Getting through all I did take everything from me and then some.

I am grateful for the lessons I have learned, the love I have felt, and the life I now have. None of this would be as it is without the battle I had to fight. It remains to be a constant fight for my life. I still experience highs and lows and have to manage and maintain a life with balance.

I know I have to be on medication for the rest of my life. This was a tough reality to face. In the process of coming to terms with my new reality, I was concerned about my bodies physical health. I wondered what my physical body would have to endure for the sake of my mental health. Nutrition and supplementation drew me in.

As a little girl, my mom always gave us vitamins. I think she was a head of her time. I knew that I had to educate myself on food and nutrition. I wanted to prevent any possible long-term effects that my medicine may cause. I found my doctors were out of touch with nutrition. They do not like to be questioned. So, I realized I had to teach myself. When it comes down to it, I know my body better than anyone else.

Having the life I do, I can recognize that I have isolated myself from the extended world around me. For a long time, I have only interacted with others when I had to. With this cocoon like existence, I didn't allow anyone else in. I only have a small circle of friends. That gets lonely at times. I have my family and my beloved, but no true girlfriends. As I started to feel more stable I realized I wanted friends in my life, but maybe not the skills to do so. To put me out there, to new environments frightens me to the bone.

I decided that starting studies with Institute of Integrative Nutrition would be my coming out. I was going to put myself out there to make friends and interact openly with the world around me. It has not been easy. I take a baby step and I do so slowly.

Looking back at my life, I can see how social settings often felt awkward. Sure, I was in open view, but cringing inside. I always had a secret I was keeping or something to be ashamed of, I thought. These kept me away from real relationships. I was fearful I would be judged or not accepted. So, I kept people and relationships at arms-length.

I really enjoyed the Institute for Integrative Nutrition. I learned how to keep my body healthy. I learned how to look at food as medicine. I learned the importance of not just what I put in my mouth, but everything else that surrounds me. I learned that all of this will also help my mental health.

I truly know that I am not my illness. I have bipolar disorder, I am not bipolar disorder!

Acknowledgements

Amber Blouch Watters, I am so happy to have you as my sister to go through all the craziness of life that we have together. I would not have made it through the throes of my illness without you. You saved my life more than once, honestly. You fought for me when I couldn't fight for myself. Thank you for blessing me with a beautiful niece and a brilliant nephew to experience unconditional love for. Dad, your tough love pushed me through even in my defiance. Thank you for being there even when it was too hard to be. Mom, you have always been my daily phone call, sometimes 2 and 3 times. You have always understood without judgement. Thank you for loving me even when I couldn't love myself. Derek Perini, my loving cousin always there with loving and encouraging support. Uncle Jim Moore, thank you for teaching me that we all do the best we can with the tools we have been given. Rob, my older brother who has gone before his time, you were always so proud of me and my education. You always told people I was your "smart" sister. You really were the glue that held us together as siblings. Tonya, so many years wasted from misbeliefs. Anna, thank you for your encouraging words in telling me I need to "know my story", and "who I am". I know. Amy, having you as an accountability partner has made all the difference. Your loving support is more than I could have dreamed. Kim. Thank you for helping me make this come alive. My Newfie Family, always ready with an embrace and unwavering support no matter what the path may be. I am very grateful for the physicians who help get me through the rough patches.

My personal favorite Poem by: Robert Frost

"Whose woods these are I think I know.

His house is in the village though;

He will not see me stopping here

To watch his woods fill up with snow.

My little horse must think it queer

To stop without a farmhouse near

Between the woods and frozen lake

The darkest evening of the year.

He gives his harness bells a shake

To ask if there is some mistake.

The only other sound's the sweep

Of easy wind and downy flake.

The woods are lovely, dark and deep,

But I have promises to keep,

And miles to go before I sleep

And miles to go before I sleep."

Brandi is available for speaking engagements.

You can reach her at:

Nourishyoursweetspot.com or

(860)410-6343

Brandi offers individual and group programs for Health Coaching.

Brandi would appreciate a review on Amazon when you have finished reading the book.

Thank you.

Resources

American Association of Suicidology

4201 Connecticut Ave. NW, Ste.408

Washington, DC

(202)237-2280

www.suicidology.org

American Foundation for Suicide Prevention

120 Wall St., 22'nd floor

New York, NY

(888)333-2377

www.afsp.org

Child and Adolescent Bipolar Foundation

www.cabf.org

DBSA – Depression & Bipolar Alliance

55 E. Jackson Blvd., Ste. 490

Chicago, Illinois

(800)826-3632

National Alliance on Mental Illness (NAMI)

3803 N. Fairfax Dr., Ste. 100

Arlington, Va.

(703)524-7600

www.nami.org

National Institute of Mental Health

6001 Executive Blvd.

Bethesda, MD

(800)421-4211

www.nimh.nih.gov

National Mental Health Association

1201 Prince St.

Alexandria, Va.

(800)969-6642

www.nmha.org

Bibliography

9/23/2017 | Jordan Younger, et al. "Gut Health." Mindbodygreen,
www.mindbodygreen.com/tag/gut-health.

Axe. "15 Brain Foods to Boost Focus and Memory." Draxe.com, Draxe,
draxe.com/health-
articles+15+brain+foods+to+boost+focus+and+memory.

"Bipolar Disorder." Psyweb.com, 9 Jan. 2017,
www.psyweb.com/Mdisorder/Mood+Dis/bipolar1.jsp+Bipolar+Diso
rde++January+9,+2017.

Cohen, Suzy. Drug Muggers: Which Medications Are Robbing Your
Body of Essential Nutrients--and Natural Ways to Restore Them.
Rodale, 2011.

Cooper, Carley. "How Food Changed Bipolar Disorder for
Me." International Bipolar Foundation, ibpf.org/blog/how-food-changed-
bipolar-disorder-me.

"ECT: Treating Severe Depression." Mayo Clinic, Mayo Foundation for
Medical Education and Research, 9 May 2017,
www.mayoclinic.org/tests-procedures/electroconvulsive-
therapy/basics/definition/PRC-20014161.

Hancock, Ka. "Bipolar Disorder and Remission." Bipolar Burble Blog | Natasha Tracy, 10 May 2013, www.natashatracy.com/illness-issues/bipolar-disorder.

Kelly, Vick. "Bipolar Illness and Capacity for Intimacy." Behavior Online, 4 Aug. 1996, www.behavior.net/forums/archives.

Lane, Cheryl. Diagnostic and Statistical Manual of Mental Disorders: DSM-5. American Psychiatric Association, 2013.

"List of Psychiatric Medications by Condition Treated." Wikipedia, Wikimedia Foundation, 18 Feb. 2017, en.wikipedia.org/wiki/List_of_psychiatric_medications_by_condition_treated.

"NAMI." Bipolar Disorder | NAMI: National Alliance on Mental Illness, 20 Mar. 2017, www.nami.org/Learn-More/Mental-Health-Conditions/Bipolar-Disorder.

Norman, Diana, et al. "Why Hypersexuality Is the Most Difficult Aspect of My Bipolar Disorder." The Mighty, 16 Aug. 2012, themighty.com/2017/07/bipolar-hypersexuality/.

Oliver, David. "10 Greatest Lies About Bipolar Disorder." Www.psyweb.com, 2013, www.psycweb.com/.

Oliver, David. "Bipolar Disorder and Intimacy." Bipolar Disorder Articles and Stories, www.bipolarcentral.com/articles bipolar disorder and intimacy.

Pelton, Ross. Drug-Induced Nutrient Depletion Handbook. Lexi-Comp, 2001.

"Psychoeducation." GoodTherapy.org Therapy Blog, 21 Mar. 2017, www.goodtherapy.org/blog/psychpedia/psychoeducation.

Smith, Hilary. "6 Bipolar Rules for Eating." World of Psychology, Psychcentral.com, 5 June 2011, psychcentral.com/blog/archives/2011/06/05/6-bipolar-rules-for-eating/comment-page-1/.

"What Food Cravings Are Telling You About Your Nutrition." Herbs Info, 24 Feb. 2016, www.herbs-info.com/blog/what-food-cravings-are-telling-you-about-your-nutrition.